WINNING
SOFTBALL
FOR GIRLS

MARK GOLA

Foreword by
MAUREEN DAVIES
Princeton University Head Softball Coach
and Canadian National Team Player

☑®
Facts On File, Inc.

WINNING SOFTBALL FOR GIRLS

Facts On File, Inc.
132 West 31st Street
New York NY 10001

Library of Congress Cataloging-in-Publication Data

Gola, Mark.
    Winning softball for girls / by Mark Gola
          p. cm.
    Includes bibliographical references and index.
    ISBN 0-8160-4709-X
    1. Softball for women. I. Title.
    GV881.3 .G65 2002
    796.357'8—dc21
    2002002493

Facts On File books are available at special discounts when purchased in bulk quantities for businesses, associations, institutions, or sales promotions. Please call our Special Sales Department in New York at (212) 967-8800 or (800) 322-8755.

You can find Facts On File on the World Wide Web at
http://www.factsonfile.com

Text design by Erika K. Arroyo
Cover design by Nora Wertz

Printed in the United States of America

VB FOF 10 9 8 7 6 5 4 3 2

This book is printed on acid-free paper.

To the Norris family,

Randy, Carol, Robyn, Dave, and Kerry

The only thing that could possibly eclipse our past on Woosamonsa Road is the future that lies ahead.

CONTENTS

5 PITCHING   97

FOREWORD

I was born into a "ball-crazy" family in Thornhill, Ontario, Canada, and grew up with a softball in my hand. Some of my fondest childhood memories were the hours spent with my family playing catch in the front yard. Little did I know then that those innocent tosses would ignite a fulfilling softball career.

What started as a pastime with family and neighborhood friends grew into year-round softball training and competition. With the encouragement and support of my parents, I played for a competitive summer-league team and traveled all over Canada and the United States. Playing with players of advanced talent improved my individual skills. My competitive zeal blossomed. The game was still fun, but I was progressing and learning the nuances of the game provided a competitive advantage. There were so many great games to speak of during those summers, but what I treasure most was the friendships that developed along the way.

Selecting a college was one of the biggest decisions of my life. When I chose Princeton University, I was able to combine my passion for softball and desire for top-level academics. The Tigers played Division-I softball in the Ivy League. The pinnacle of my collegiate career was playing in the 1995 and 1996 Women's College World Series. We faced the best players and teams in America, all the while representing Princeton University women's softball.

My wonderful experience as a student-athlete at Princeton allowed me to pursue my dream of playing softball at an even higher level. As a result of years of hard work and discipline, I had the honor of playing with the Canadian national softball team from 1996–2001. There are few feelings that rival the emotions spurred by competing for your country. I will never forget the feeling of putting on my Team Canada jersey for the first time and every time thereafter.

During the last decade, women's fast-pitch softball has made tremendous strides in becoming a competitive sport throughout the world. It was introduced as an official Olympic sport in the 1996 Olympic Games in Atlanta. Its successful debut on a global stage created enough energy and excitement to improve play on an international scale. The progress of the sport was evident during the 2000 Olympics in Sydney when the traditionally dominant United States national team found its defense of the gold medal in jeopardy.

Although they eventually repeated as gold medal champions in Sydney, their path to the gold was far more challenging and dramatic than their undefeated run in 1996.

In the summer of 2000, I began a new chapter in my softball career. I was named the new head softball coach at Princeton University. While I now look at the game through the eyes of a coach, my passion for softball is as strong as ever. It's true that softball is just a game, but it encompasses much more than throwing, hitting, and catching a ball. Lessons learned on the field such as teamwork, responsibility, respect, discipline, perseverance, motivation, and determination prove invaluable to building individual character. And they are qualities applicable to everyday life. Now it is my turn to give something back to the game that has shaped and defined me.

I often think back to those days of playing catch with my family. That is where it all began for me. And it can begin there for you too. Learning the basics are the building blocks that can lead to unlimited opportunities in the sport and beyond. *Winning Softball for Girls* is an excellent tool that will help players and coaches learn the fundamentals of the game. I wish I had this book to read and refer to when I was developing my game. It presents a sound basis of information and instruction that will undoubtedly improve aspiring players. It will help them attain their personal goals and realize their greatest dreams.

If you want to be the best, start with reading *Winning Softball for Girls*. You'll be on your way. And perhaps you'll enjoy your days on the softball field as much as I have enjoyed mine.

—Maureen Davies
Princeton University softball head coach
and former member of the Canadian national team

ACKNOWLEDGMENTS

First, I'd like to thank Randy Voorhees, for developing the proposal for this book, selling it, and suggesting that I write it. If good ideas could be cashed at the bank, Randy would have to worry about nothing more than which ballgame to watch and where he left his last tin of Skoal.

Thanks to James Chambers at Facts On File, for his continued support and belief in this series.

I'm greatly appreciative of the efforts of Princeton University head coach Maureen Davies for writing the foreword and reviewing the manuscript. Maureen was instrumental in making sure the information was accurate in content and presentation. Her assistant coach at Princeton, Jennifer Sewell, was also very helpful in contributing her knowledge and expertise to the manuscript.

As always, photographer Mike Plunkett did an exceptional job taking all the stop-action photographs for this book. Thanks also to Margaret Trejo for creating the diagrams.

Thanks to the gifted young softball players who modeled in the photo shoot: Corey Bowker, Serena Fleming, Eliza Kelemen, Tara Harrigan, Jessica Williams, Lindsey Williams, Kristen Zabawa. These girls are a fine representation of the outstanding new generation of talent in fast-pitch softball. A special thanks to Eliza Kelemen for organizing the group of players and her friendship.

Thanks to Rick Freeman, Rider University assistant baseball coach, friend and traveling roommate, for not growing irritated while I typed away on a laptop in hotel rooms during our weekend conference trips.

Thanks to John Monteleone, President of Mountain Lion, Inc., and Joan Mohan, office manager at Mountain Lion, for their contributions to this book.

Finally, thanks to my parents, Edward and Paulette Gola, brother Ed Gola, and my good buddy Norm Coryell.

INTRODUCTION

The very best athletes seek perfection, and pursue it with desire, dedication, tenacity, and perseverance. But in truth, a softball player can never be perfect. There is always an area of one's game that can be improved. Batters can improve by eliminating weaknesses or enhancing their power and consistency at the plate. Pitchers can add a new pitch to their repertoire or become more proficient at setting up hitters. Baserunners can upgrade their speed and quickness, or tighten up their angles rounding bases. All facets of a player's game can be improved, no matter how accomplished they are. That's what makes fast-pitch softball so exciting. There is no limit to how good you can be.

Two factors lead to improvement. The first is knowledge. A player has to understand the proper technique or method of play to emulate those correct actions on the field. You can't improve your throwing unless you know and comprehend the mechanics and artistry of throwing. The second factor is training. To perform the proper movements without thought, they must be practiced over and over again, until it becomes second nature. The goal is to develop muscle memory, which means your body automatically performs the correct action immediately upon receiving a message from the brain.

This book, *Winning Softball for Girls*, provides the reader with the "how to" as well as the "how to improve." The basic fundamentals of each skill are discussed in detail and illustrated with photographs. Advanced skills are also presented to offer valuable information to those who aspire to compete at the highest levels of play.

Because hitting and pitching are so essential to fast-pitch softball, they are given the greatest depth of treatment. Hitters will learn the proper mechanics of the swing as they are broken down piece by piece, giving each step of the swing full attention. Other aspects of hitting such as learning the strike zone and hitting zone, mastering situational hitting, developing confidence, and avoiding (or troubleshooting) the ten most common faults are also included.

No position in fast-pitch softball carries greater importance than the performance of the pitcher. As is often said, good pitching always beats good hitting. The windmill delivery is fully discussed, so young pitchers can understand the fundamentally sound delivery. This special chapter teaches the reader how to grip and throw various pitches like fastballs, change-ups, drop pitches, curveballs, and riseballs. The chapter also suggests the optimum situations in which to throw these pitches. Poise, preparation, confidence, and setting up hitters are intangible skills that successful pitchers possess—these are examined and discussed.

Chapter 3: The Fundamentals of Fielding, gives basic instruction on throwing, catching, fielding ground balls, and catching fly balls. Chapter 4: The Positions, reviews the responsibility of each defensive position on the field. Playing the third-base position, for example, entails much more than fielding balls that are hit to third base. These duties are explained in this chapter.

The treatment is rounded out with chapters that offer tips and advice in baserunning, offensive and defensive strategy, and conditioning. The introductory chapter—History, Rules and Equipment—surveys the growth of fast-pitch softball and how the game functions today. Because strength and conditioning have become essential to a young athlete's growth and development, special attention was given to Chapter 9: Body Conditioning. This section of the book includes information on weight training, cardiovascular training, agility training, and nutrition.

Several drills and games are provided at the end of each chapter. These exercises are tailored to improve specific skills. As mentioned, it's important for athletes and coaches to understand the "how to," but they should also seek out methods of "how to improve." These drills and games will train the body to execute the correct movements, and develop the muscle memory that is so important in order to become a productive player in competitive situations.

By absorbing and then practicing the information presented in *Winning Softball for Girls*, the reader will become a better, smarter, more efficient softball player. After you've finished reading this book, keep it in a special place so you can go back and review or refer to it in times of need. Reading and applying the advice in this book clearly illustrates your dedication and determination to becoming a better player. If you train hard and devote the necessary time to practicing and improving your game, in our book, you're already a winner.

—Mark Gola

1

HISTORY, RULES, AND EQUIPMENT

HISTORY

In November of 1887, Chicago reporter George W. Hancock stumbled upon the idea of playing a game of indoor baseball. While a group of Yale and Harvard alumni were looking for a diversion from the blustery winter weather, a Yale student picked up a boxing glove and fired it at a Harvard alumnus. He, in turn, attempted to hit the glove back with a stick. A light bulb went off in Hancock's head and he suggested that they make a game out of it.

Hancock quickly tied together the laces of the boxing glove for a ball, marked a home plate, bases, and a pitcher's box with a piece of chalk, and divided the group into two teams. The teams battled each other and the first-ever softball game ended in a 41–40 score. Later that spring, Hancock moved the game outdoors, appending 19 rules to adapt the outdoor game from the indoor game.

The game began to spread throughout the country, but grew rapidly in Minneapolis in 1895 when Louis Rober, a Minneapolis Fire Department lieutenant, adopted the game to keep his firemen fit during their idle time. Using a vacant lot, Rober created a field with a pitching distance at 35 feet. The game rapidly became popular as other fire companies began to compete. Roberts soon transferred to another company and brought the game with him. Today, more than 40 million people play recreational softball, making it the number one participant sport in the United States.

In 1933, the Amateur Softball Association (ASA), founded by Leo Fischer and Michael J. Pauley, was formed to govern and promote softball in the United States. The ASA set up a committee that established one set of rules now used by teams in all parts of the world. The International Softball Federation, founded in 1952, governs international competition. It has more than 70 member nations, whose teams compete in annual regional, national, and international tournaments.

Fast-pitch softball in the United States is a sport played predominantly by women. Popularized by pioneers such as Joan Joyce, Debbie Doom, and Dot Richardson, women's fast-pitch softball has exploded in America and is now the fourth most popular sport played by high school girls. More than 343,000 girls play high school softball each year and over 17,000 girls compete at the collegiate level. The ASA now annually registers 245,000 softball teams, which house more than 1.2 million girls.

In recent years, women's fast-pitch softball has experienced a new form of popularity. By being accepted as an official team sport in the 1996 Olympics, women's fast-pitch softball gained significant exposure. The American national team took the spotlight and finally received publicity as an international powerhouse. In the 1996 Summer Olympics in Atlanta, the United States women won the first-ever Olympic gold medal in fast-pitch softball. Four years later, they repeated as Olympic champions by earning the gold medal during the 2000 Summer Olympics in Sydney.

Today, names such as Dot Richardson, Lisa Fernandez, Sheila Douty, Michele Granger, and Christa Williams are recognized by Americans throughout the country. By following in the footsteps of their predecessors, young girls can aspire to become national team representatives and Olympic stars in the sport of fast-pitch softball.

RULES

The following rules were selected as the most essential rules of the game.

The Field

The softball field consists of an infield diamond and an outfield territory that may or may not be enclosed by a fence. Four bases that mark the diamond are 60 feet apart. The distance of the outfield fence varies, but the recommended dimensions are 200 feet down the foul lines and 205 feet to center field. The pitching distance is 40 feet in high school, national, and international competition. The pitching distance is 43 feet in collegiate fast-pitch softball.

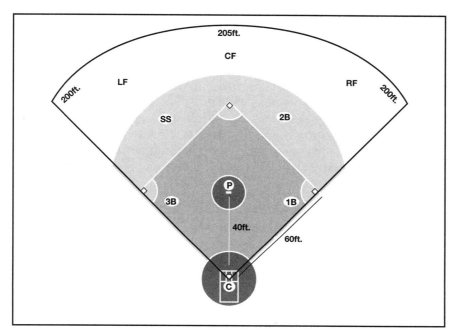

This diagram illustrates the basic field positioning of each player. The distance from the pitching rubber to home plate is 40 feet, except in collegiate competition where it is moved back to 43 feet.

HOME PLATE
The home plate is made of rubber or other suitable material. It is 17 inches wide and $8^1/2$ inches deep.

PITCHING RUBBER
The pitching rubber is made of rubber and is level with the ground. It is two feet wide and six inches deep. The pitching rubber is placed in the middle of the pitching circle, which is 16 feet in diameter.

BASES
The bases are made of canvas or other suitable material. Bases are 15 inches long by 15 inches wide. The bases must be securely fastened in position for fairness and to avoid risk of injury.

The Game

A game consists of seven innings. A full seven innings do not have to be played if the second batting team (the home team) scores more runs before the third player is out in the last half of the seventh inning. A tied game continues into "extra innings" until one side has scored more runs at the end of a completed inning, or if the home team scores more runs before their half of the inning before the third out.

A game is official if five innings are completed or if the home team has scored more runs before the third player is out in the last half of the fifth inning. Games are often called due to poor weather conditions or darkness. If the game does not reach official status, it is either resumed from the point of its interruption at a later scheduled date or started over from the beginning. This condition is agreed upon before the start of the contest by each team's coaches.

TEAMS

Each team consists of nine players on the field when playing defense. The defensive positions are as follows: pitcher, catcher, first baseman, second baseman, third baseman, shortstop, left fielder, right fielder, center fielder. Pitchers and catchers must stand in their prescribed positions. Other players cover specific territories in the field, but may adjust their positioning depending on the batter or game situation.

On offense, each of the nine players on the field gets a turn to bat in the line-up. A tenth player, called a designated hitter, may also be added to the line-up. Including a designated hitter in the line-up is optional.

Players bat in the order listed on the line-up card. This called the "batting line-up." If a player has not completed a turn at bat when her team's half of the inning at bat has ended, she becomes the first batter of the next inning at bat.

SCORING

The winning team is the one that scores the most runs. A run is scored when a player safely completes a circuit around the bases, touching each base in turn before arriving at home plate.

OUTS

An out is declared by the umpire and indicates that an offensive player has been retired. Each team is entitled three outs per inning. A force out is a put out during which an offensive player who is being forced to advance is tagged out, or is put out by a fielder who holds the ball while touching the base toward which the forced runner is advancing. A tag out is putting out an offensive player, who is not touching a base, by touching the runner with a live ball or with the glove or hand when the live ball is securely held by a fielder.

A batter is out if a ball is legally caught on the fly; if the ball is popped up to the infield with less than two outs and there are runners on first and second, or first, second, and third base (infield fly rule); the preceding runner interferes with an attempt to field the ball. There are three strikes against the batter when fewer than two teammates are out and the first base is occupied, and the third strike is caught by the catcher; the batter misses the third strike and is hit by the ball; the batter bunts the third strike into foul territory.

A runner is out when she is forced out; tagged out; when having left a base before a fly ball is caught, the runner fails to return to that base before it or the runner is tagged by a fielder with the ball; running more than three feet from a direct line between the bases to avoid being tagged out (running out of the baseline); overtaking a preceding runner; deliberately interfering with an attempt to field the ball or with a thrown ball; being hit by a fair ball off base before the ball has touched or passed a fielder.

STRIKE ZONE

The strike zone is the area over any part of home plate, which is between the batter's armpit and the top of the knees when the batter assumes a natural batting stance. The umpire shall determine the batter's strike zone if they're employing an unusual batting stance.

A strike is called when the ball enters the strike zone and the batter does not swing, or if the batter swings and misses. A batted ball landing in foul territory is also a strike. Each batter is allowed three strikes. A ball is a ball pitched outside of the strike zone and not swung at by the batter.

Pitching

The pitcher must stand with both feet touching the pitching rubber. She must face the batter with her shoulders aligned with first and third base, holding the ball in front of her body. The delivery starts when one hand is taken off the ball. The pitcher may take one step that must be forward, toward the batter, and simultaneous with the delivery. Any step backward shall begin before the hands come together.

The pivot foot may remain in contact with or may push off and drag away from the pitching rubber prior to the front foot touching the ground, as a long as the pivot foot remains in contact with the ground and within the two-foot width of the pitching rubber.

The ball must be delivered underhand, and the hand must be below the hip, with the wrist no farther from the body than the elbow. The release of the ball and the follow-through of the hand and wrist must be in a forward direction, past the straight line of the body. There should be no more than one revolution in a windmill delivery.

PITCHING INFRACTIONS

- Any infraction is an illegal pitch. The ball is dead at the end of the playing action. The batter is awarded a ball and base runners are awarded one base without liability to be put out.
- The pitcher shall not deliberately drop, roll, or bounce the ball while in pitching position.
- The pitcher shall not use tape or any other substance on the ball or contact points of the pitching hand or fingers. A pitcher who licks her fingers must wipe them off before bringing them into contact with the ball.
- Once the ball is returned to the pitcher, she has 20 seconds to release the next pitch.
- If the ball slips from the pitcher's hand during the backswing or forward motion, a ball is called on the batter. The ball remains in play and runners may advance at their own risk.
- The pitcher shall not throw to a base while her foot is in contact with the pitching rubber after having taken the pitcher's position.

Batting

Each player on the team gets a turn to become the batter. The batter takes her position in the batter's box (on either side) in the order in which she appears on the line-up card as delivered to the umpire prior to the game. This order shall be followed throughout the game unless a substitute is summoned to replace a player during the game. The substitute will bat in that player's spot in the line-up.

A strike is charged to a batter when a pitched ball enters any part of the strike zone in flight and is not swung at; a pitched ball is swung at and missed; a pitched ball is hit foul when the batter has less than two strikes; a pitched ball is hit foul on an attempted bunt; a penalty strike is called because the batter fails to take her position in the batter's box within 20 seconds; a batted ball makes contact with the batter in the batter's box.

A ball is credited to the batter when a pitch is not touched by the bat and is not a strike, when there is an illegal pitch, or for a catcher's or pitcher's delay.

The batter must stay within the area of the batter's box during her turn at bat. She must be within that area during her stance, stride, and swing. If at any time the batter's feet fall outside of the batter's box, she is called out. The batter's box is three feet wide by five feet deep.

Running

The batter becomes a runner upon hitting the ball into fair territory, after four balls, after interference by the catcher, when a pitch strikes the batter, and when a fair ball strikes an umpire. A runner may move to the next base while the ball is in play, when the ball leaves the pitcher's hand, when the ball is overthrown, and when the ball is batted into play.

The runner may also advance to the next base when the batter is awarded a base and preceding bases are occupied, when a fielder obstructs a runner, when a fielder illegally stops a ball, and when the ball is overthrown into foul territory and ruled out of play.

Runners must return to their bases when a ball is legally caught on the fly, when the ball is batted illegally, after interference by a batter or runner, and when the batter is hit by a pitched ball and the preceding bases are unoccupied.

EQUIPMENT

Uniforms

Uniforms of all team members should be of the same color and style. The school's official uniform (including uniform jersey, and/or shorts/pants, visible undergarments, stockings, socks, caps, or headwear) may bear only a single manufacturer's logo or trademark that does not exceed $2^1/4$ square inches. A number on the back of each player's jersey is required and should be at least six inches high. The number must be of a solid color contrasting with the color of the shirt. One American flag may be worn on each item of uniform apparel.

Head Gear

Caps, visors, or headbands may be worn but they must all be the same color. Uniform sleeve lengths may vary, but the sleeves of each individual player should be approximately the same length and shall not be ragged, frayed, or slit.

A batting helmet is mandatory for each batter, on-deck batter, base runners, and players in the coach's boxes. The batting helmet shall have extended earflaps that cover both ears and temples. Batting helmets that are broken, cracked, dented, or that have been altered are prohibited from use.

The catcher shall wear a head protector and a protective mask with a throat protector that is part of or attached to the mask. A catcher should also wear a body protector and protective shin guards. Failure to wear the required catcher's equipment when ordered to do so by the umpire results in the player to be ejected from the game.

Ball

The ball should be a white or yellow optic sphere formed by solid core or number one long-fiber Kapok or yarn, wound around a small cork or rubber and covered with a flat surface or a smooth seam stitch which is not visible. The ball should weigh no less than $6^1/4$ ounces and no more than seven ounces.

Bat

The bats should be a smooth cylinder with a knob. A bat cannot be more than $2^1/4$ inches in diameter at its thickest part and no more than 34 inches in length. A bat shall have a safety grip of cork, tape, or composition material. The grip shall extend a minimum of 10 inches, but no more than 15 inches, from the handle end of the bat.

Gloves

Gloves should be worn by all fielders and (except the catcher) shall conform to the following maximum specifications. The height measured from the bottom edge or heel straight up across the center of the palm, to a line even with the highest point of the glove should be 14 inches. The width of the palm measured from the bottom edge of the webbing farthest from the thumb in a horizontal line, to the outside of the little finger edge of the glove should be eight inches. The webbing measured across the top end or along any line parallel to the top should be $5^3/4$ inches.

Footwear

Players are required to wear athletic shoes. Shoe sole or heel protections other than the standard shoe plate are prohibited. Metal cleats and metal toe plates are prohibited.

2
HITTING

AUTHOR'S ADMONITION

Because hitting is the most popular and widely practiced skill in softball, this chapter will draw considerable attention. I'd like to speak briefly to the young readers anxious to learn the vital components of the swing.

The following chapter presents an abundance of information about hitting. Each step of the swing is discussed in detail. To acquire knowledge about this particular aspect of the game is extremely beneficial, but only when it is applied at the appropriate time. Do not foster thoughts about the mechanics of the swing while you're at the plate. Cluttering your head with too many thoughts can prove detrimental to your performance. Game-time at bats are a time for reaction and execution. Allow your muscle memory to control your swing.

Practice and individual hitting sessions present opportune times to refine your mechanics. Iron out the flaws in your stance, pre-swing, swing, or follow through by using the drills recommended in this chapter. Once you've established a fundamentally sound swing, repeat the swing thousands of times to ingrain the correct physical movements into your brain. Once that is accomplished, it simply becomes a matter of getting a good pitch and blasting it into orbit.

Every time you lace up your cleats and run out onto an athletic field, your primary goal should be enjoyment. Regardless of the sport,

Hitting is a combination of timing, technique, and confidence.

having fun is what it's all about. Sure there are ups and downs throughout the course of a game or season, but if you're not out there to have fun, it's time to find a new interest.

In softball, no aspect of the game is more fun than hitting. It's the hot fudge on your ice cream sundae, the study hall in your class schedule. Hitting is a craft never perfected, but constantly explored and practiced. It can be frustrating and very humbling, but when performed successfully, it is exhilarating. The feeling of the ball meeting the sweet spot of the bat is an addictive one, and it leaves such a sweet flavor that it keeps hitters hungry for each pitch they're served.

There are no shortcuts in your travels toward becoming a good hitter. It requires constant practice. You must hit thousands upon thousands of balls to develop good hand-to-eye coordination. You must see countless pitches to develop timing, rhythm, and an adept knowledge of the strike zone. You must take hundreds of thousands of swings to refine your mechanics and develop the muscle memory. Muscle memory occurs when your body performs an action without thought. When you rise from your chair and walk to the door, you don't think about the steps you're taking. You *"just do it."* Muscle memory is necessary to perform instinctively in the game. Finally, you must endure all of the above to build the confidence that will enable you to relax at the plate and swing the bat with authority.

There is a silver lining to all the effort it takes to become a good hitter. Although hitting is an enterprise that requires more practice than any other trait, it's the most fun. While many players would describe extra baserunning practice as a tedious or tiresome exercise, extra batting practice is a welcome affair.

So dig in and take your hacks, that is, if the pitcher serves you one over the plate.

CONFIDENCE

Before discussing the fundamentals of hitting, let's first talk about an element that all good hitters possess: confidence. As golf legend Jack Nicklaus once said, "Confidence breeds success." Whether it's at the youth league, high school, or Olympic level of play, good hitters believe they are good hitters. They never walk up to the plate *hoping* to hit the ball hard, they *know* they are going to hit the ball hard. To make consistent, solid contact, you must believe in yourself.

Preparation

A major factor in developing confidence is preparation. If you're prepared heading into competition, you'll feel self-assured and set lofty goals. When you're unprepared, you feel insecure and lower your expectations. Always remember positive thoughts produce positive results.

Think about taking a math test or science test in school. Studying not only prepares you to answer questions about the material, but it also improves your mental health entering the exam. You become confident that you'll score favorably. If you don't study, you'll be unsure of yourself. You'll be nervous and indecisive. Individuals do not perform at their best when they're concerned. They perform best when they're confident.

How do you prepare? Swings, swings, and more swings. There are many drills we'll discuss later in this chapter that will refine your mechanics, accelerate your bat speed, improve your judgment of the strike zone, and eliminate swing faults. Executing those drills religiously will prepare you for gametime.

Quiet Confidence

Part of being a good athlete is learning to handle success. All good athletes are confident in their abilities, but they restrain themselves from showcasing that confidence. Confidence is a feeling, not an exhibition. Respected athletes carry quiet confidence. They have it, but feel no need to put it on display.

Cockiness can be an athlete's Achilles' heel in sports. Not only does it cast a negative light on your character, but it also detracts from your awareness. You must respect your opponent and focus on what it takes to defeat them. If you spend your time thinking of yourself and how great you are, someone will knock you off your high horse. Never take your opponent lightly. Approach your competitors with respect.

Maintaining Confidence

Hitting can often be as unpredictable as the weather. There are stretches where you hit every pitch on the button. The softball appears to be as big as a watermelon as it approaches home plate and your confidence is sky-high. At other times, the ball seems as small as a grape and the hits come few and far between. This is when it's most important to maintain your level of confidence. Refer back to when times were going well and visualize those hard-hit balls. Understand that even the very best hitters struggle at the plate and you simply must work hard to get back on track.

Remember, when you're experiencing a rainy day, think back to when the sun was shining and avoid the possibility of a week-long storm.

FIVE MENTAL TIPS TO LIVE BY

1. Confidence is the foundation of a good hitter.
2. Preparation fuels your confidence.
3. Never hope to get a hit. Know you're going to get a hit.
4. Confidence allows you flourish; cockiness creates weaknesses.
5. To be a clutch hitter, you've got to embrace clutch situations.

THE GRIP

To understand and execute the proper fundamentals of hitting, you've got to start at the ground level. A proper grip may seem simple and basic, but it's extremely important to your swing. It enables you to handle the bat with power, control, and smoothness. An incorrect grip causes a host of problems that produce inefficient swings.

When taking your grip, your right hand rests on top of your left hand. The top of the left hand should touch the bottom of the right hand. There is no visible space between the hands. This allows your hands to work as a single unit. In hitting, your hands must work together to yield success.

Let the Fingers Do the Talking

The bat is held primarily in the fingers. Many young players mistakenly lay the bat in their palms, but this is incorrect. The handle should lie across the line created by where the bottom of your fingers meet the top of your palm. To start, open your right hand so the palm faces up and place the handle of the bat across the line in your top. Next, do the same with your left hand and fold both sets of fingers over the handle. Both hands are now gripping the bat in the fingers. If you feel the handle resting deep in your palms or down near your thumbs, move it up into your fingers.

Why should the bat lie in the fingers? More strength lies in your fingers. To feel this, grab your left wrist with your right hand. First, place only your finger pads on your wrist and lift your palm up off the wrist. Squeeze your wrist with your fingers as hard as you can. Next, do the opposite. Press your palm against your wrist and lift your fingers up off the wrist. Now try squeezing. You have considerably less strength, don't you? Not only less strength, but less control. Keep the handle of the bat in your fingers to maximize the strength, quickness, and control of your swing.

PICKING A BAT THAT WORKS FOR *YOU*

Choosing a bat that works for you depends on your height and strength. Don't select a bat simply based on age or what your friend is using.

At the store, look for a bat that comes up to the top of your leg or just above it. If it extends up to your waist or belt line, it may be too long. A bat that goes up to your thigh is probably too short. Also consider where you take your batting stance. With your arms just short of full extension, look at where the barrel hovers over home plate. If it's over the middle of the plate, the length is a good fit.

When searching for the right weight, grab several bats of varying weights. Swing each bat and find the heaviest one that you're able to swing at top speed. If the barrel feels a little heavy or tends to drag when you swing it, try a lighter bat. Do not make the mistake of buying a bat that is too light. You're sacrificing power.

Take mom or dad along with you to the store. Ask them to watch you swing the bat and help pick out the heaviest bat that you can swing at optimum speed.

Align the Knuckles

In each hand are three sets of knuckles. The first set is located near your fingertips. The second set is in the middle of your fingers and the third set is at the top of your palm.

When gripping the bat, the middle knuckles of the top hand line up slightly to the left of the middle knuckles of the bottom hand. (This description is from the batter's viewpoint.) A common mistake to avoid is lining up the middle knuckles of the top hand with the third set of knuckles of your bottom hand. This grip produces a top-hand dominant swing. You'll pull every pitch, most of which will result in ground balls. The top and bottom hand must work as one, single unit in order to hit the ball to all fields.

Eliminate the Tension

Have you ever watched a world-class sprinter like Marion Jones or Gail Devers run their race? If so, you may have noticed their faces are loose and relaxed as they're running. There is no tension in their bodies. To perform at maximum speed, power, and control, athletes must eliminate tension completely.

Hold the bat in your fingers, not the palms. Check the alignment of your knuckles. The middle set of knuckles of your top hand should be aligned with, or slightly past, the middle set of knuckles of your bottom hand.

Tension is the enemy of a hitter. It reduces bat speed (the pace at which the hitter swings the bat), diminishes power, and decreases bat control. The grip is where tension often originates, so make sure your hands remain free of tension. Apply enough pressure with your fingers so you can hold the bat steadily, but do not squeeze the bat with a death grip. Many Olympic softball players allow their fingers to flicker on and off the handle as they await the pitch. This keeps the hands loose and staves off tension.

THE STANCE

Every hitter employs her own unique stance in the batter's box. Some are very basic, while others are a bit quirky. It's a matter of personal preference. What works for Dot Richardson may not work for Lisa Fernandez, and what works for Lisa Fernandez may not work for you.

A Workable, Comfortable Stance

When trying to find a stance that suits you, keep two simple rules in mind: your stance must be comfortable and it must be workable. If you live by those two guidelines, your stance will suffice.

Comfort is very important. Your stance in the batter's box is the basic foundation from which you'll execute your swing and if you're not comfortable using it, it's not going to yield success. Much like lounging on the couch, being comfortable means you're relaxed and you've got to be relaxed at the plate. If you're not, tension will become a factor.

A stance that is workable means it doesn't hinder your ability to make an easy transition from the stance to the stride and swing. For example, say you hold your hands high in your stance up around your head. If this hand position does not affect your swing and its timing, then it's okay. If, however, it's making you late on pitches because you have to first lower your hands before you can start your swing, then you have to make a change. There is some flexibility in how you set up your stance, but not so much that it negatively affects your swing.

The Textbook Stance

To develop proper fundamentals, simplicity is the best path to follow. All young hitters should begin with a basic stance. First, place the bat on the ground and get into the *athletic position.* The athletic position means your feet are positioned slightly farther than shoulder-width apart. The knees are flexed and you're slightly bent at the waist. If you play other sports, the athletic position is a very familiar pose. In basketball, it's the position a player takes when guarding the dribble. In tennis, imagine the player who awaits the serve. In soccer, think of the

A basic batting stance is not much different than the traditional athletic position. Feet are spread slightly farther than shoulder-width, the knees are flexed, and weight is on the balls of your feet.

goalkeeper preparing to stop a shot. In each of these sports, the athlete is bent at the waist, knees flexed and feet spread a bit more than shoulder-width apart.

The most important element of the athletic position is that you carry your weight on the balls of your feet. This affords balance. Do not lean forward onto your toes or backward onto your heels. Stay on the balls of your feet to create a rock-solid base.

The importance of balance in the stance and swing cannot be underestimated. Maintaining balance from start to finish places you in the strongest possible position to hit the ball. Also, keeping your body under control enables your eyes to track the pitch with greater ease.

Using the proper grip, grab the bat and hold it just off your rear shoulder. The handle should be approximately three to four inches away from your body. This bat position is recommended because it's close to where you'll begin your forward swing.

Weight Distribution

There is one slight variation to the athletic position when it comes to the batting stance. Instead of having your weight centered in the middle of your body, shift more weight onto your rear leg. If you're a numbers whiz, the breakdown is to have approximately 60 percent of your weight on your rear leg and 40 percent on your front leg. Feel the additional weight *inside* your rear leg. Do not lean back and allow the

From the athletic position, hold the bat just off your rear shoulder and shift approximately 60 percent of your weight onto your rear leg.

weight to leak outside your rear leg. This is a common fault that leads to overstriding (a stride that is too long).

The reason to shift more weight onto your rear leg is so you have the momentum of your lower body moving into the ball when you make contact. To generate power, the weight must start back and then move slightly forward with the swing. This movement is very subtle but extremely significant.

Stance Position

Where you plant your feet in the batter's box may depend on a variety of factors. Bunting, slap hitting, and the pitcher's repertoire are game situations that may influence your positioning. We'll wait to discuss that in Chapter 7: Offensive Strategy. What we want to focus on here is plate coverage.

Achieving full plate coverage means that you're able to contact inside, middle, and outside strikes. If you're too far from the plate, you'll be susceptible to the outside strike. Stand too close and you're giving up the inside corner. You want to find a happy medium so the

A batting stance must be comfortable and workable. Generally, the best stance to use is a simple stance.

pitcher won't be able to spot a weakness.

To check your plate coverage, stand in the batter's box. First, imagine a pitch is right down the middle, take your stride and start to swing, but stop your bat over the plate (where you would make contact). Check to make sure the barrel of the bat is over home plate. When doing this exercise, make sure you rotate your hips. If you don't, this experiment produces inaccurate results.

Next, imagine the pitch is on the outside corner. Repeat the same process but contact is made a little deeper in the strike zone (toward the back of home plate) and rotate your hips less. (These are both keys to hitting the outside strike, which will be reviewed later in this chapter.) Look to see that the barrel of the bat is over the outside part of the plate. Finally, imagine the pitch is an inside strike. Repeat the process but make sure the contact point is out in front of home plate and your hips are fully rotated. (These are both keys to hitting the inside strike that will be covered later in the chapter.) The barrel should be over the inside part of home plate.

Once you figure out how far you'll stand from home plate, establish the depth of your stance. Place your front foot in line with the middle of home plate and assume your normal-stance width (slightly farther than shoulder-width). You may adjust the depth of your stance at times during the game. Perhaps the pitcher throws very fast. In this case, stand farther back in the box. If the pitcher throws a lot of off-speed and breaking pitches, move forward in the box.

THE STRIDE

The stride is also referred to as the "step." It is your first forward movement toward the ball. Striding with the front foot widens your base and allows the lower half of the body more leverage to transmit power into your swing. It is a subtle movement made only with the lower body, and helps get things started.

Executing the stride correctly is very important because it puts you in good position from which to swing the bat forcefully. An incorrect stride can ruin a hitter, so it's worth your practice time to get it right from the start.

The stride should be a minimal, forward movement of the front foot. It's a short, soft step that travels directly at the pitcher. The length of your stride should be approximately four to six inches. A tall girl may stride a little farther than that and a smaller girl might stride a bit shorter.

The reason the stride must be soft is so you're able to keep your weight back. To get an idea of what soft means, imagine that it's wintertime and you have to walk across a stream that is frozen over. You're given the unwanted job of checking the thickness of the ice. When doing so, you would reach out lightly with your foot and apply very little pressure. If you step forcefully and allow your weight to fall forward, you might fall through. Apply this same type of timid stride at the plate.

As you take your stride, the front foot remains closed (parallel to the rubber). This keeps your hips and shoulders aligned with the

Left: The batter is set in her stance. Right: She has taken her stride. Her stride length is short and directed straight back toward the pitcher. Notice that her weight has not yet shifted forward, and is still firmly loaded on her rear leg.

This is an example of a flawed stride. She strides too far, shifting her weight forward onto her front leg. This causes her head (and eyes) to move forward. Premature weight shift also diminishes the role of the lower body, minimizing hip rotation, which reduces bat speed and power.

pitcher. All your power remains intact and ready to explode on the incoming pitch. If the front foot lands open (toe pointing at the pitcher), your hips and shoulders open prematurely. You've just lost significant power from your swing.

Timing Your Stride

The timing of your stride will vary slightly from pitcher to pitcher. That said, in most cases you'll take your stride just before the pitcher releases the ball. As the pitch is released, your stride foot is planted on the ground and you're ready to uncork your swing. Many hitters and coaches are under the misconception that you gauge the location of the pitch (inside, middle or outside) and then adjust your stride to the location of the pitch. *This is completely wrong.* There is not enough time to do this. If you wait until the pitch is released to stride, you'll be late with your swing every time. Train yourself to stride toward the pitcher each time. It enables you to hit every pitch regardless of its location.

Your timing varies slightly due to the individual pitcher's velocity and speed of motion. If she throws very hard, everything has to start a split-second earlier. If she's a control pitcher that throws slower, delay your stride so you're not at a dead standstill waiting for the ball to get to home plate.

WHY STRIDE SQUARE?

Striding square to the pitcher allows you to cover any pitch in the horizontal strike zone—inside, outside, and middle. Striding open (or away from home plate) is often referred to as stepping in the bucket. This moves your body away from home plate leaving the outside portion of the plate uncovered. Even though inside and middle strikes will be in your contact zone, your power will be diminished. Stepping in the bucket opens your hips prematurely.

Striding closed (toward home plate) enables you to hit outside strikes, but strikes on the inside corner will give you fits. When you stride closed, you block your hips. In other words, you'll tie yourself up. You won't be able to fully rotate them, which is essential to hitting inside strikes. Chances are you'll hit the ball below the barrel (get jammed), hook the ball foul or take the pitch for a called strike because it appears inside.

Striding square keeps your entire body aligned and moving toward the incoming pitch. You'll improve your power, quickness, and consistency at the plate. Hitters who are able to cover the entire plate are tough outs for pitchers. Be a tough out. Stride square.

KEY POINTS TO THE STRIDE

- Start your stride just before the pitcher releases the ball.
- Stride directly back toward the pitcher.
- The stride is a short, soft step.
- Keep your weight and hands back as the stride foot lands.
- The stride foot remains closed as it plants.

No matter where the ball is located, stride directly toward the pitcher on every pitch.

THE LAUNCH POSITION

The *launch position* is the final position the hitter sets in before she starts her forward swing to the ball. It is also called the *power position* and *ready position.* In the launch position, the stride foot is planted on the ground and the hands are cocked back just beyond the rear shoulder. All good hitters get to this position before they swing the bat. Dot Richardson, Lisa Fernandez, and Sheila Douty may have different stances, but they are all in this position after the stride foot has planted.

We discussed the stride and its importance to the swing. Getting into the launch position is equally important and it happens simultaneously with the stride. As the stride foot moves forward, the hands move back. It's a subtle movement back of about two to four inches.

Moving the hands back to the launch position is important because it gets you to "load up" before swinging the bat. With any forceful act in sports, you must go back before you move forward to gain power and quickness. When a track star makes her approach in the javelin event, she rears her throwing arm back before hurling the shaft. A field hockey player draws her stick back before hitting a powerful drive and a volleyball player cocks her arm back before delivering a spike. Moving your hands back to the launch position adds fuel to your swing.

From the stance position (left), the hands must move back while the front foot strides forward. This allows the hitter to "load up" and increase the strength of her swing.

Don't Roll and Don't Wrap

The hands move back approximately two to four inches when traveling to the launch position. Do not, however, roll your front shoulder in so much that your bat wraps behind your back. Think about pushing the hands straight back along your shoulder-line. Keep the elbows flexed as you execute this movement. The front shoulder will coil slightly inward naturally. This is okay. If you roll the front shoulder too far inward, it creates problems. The first is that your head will turn inward and you'll be peering out at the pitch with one eye. The second problem is that by rolling in, you'll move your hands too far back and behind you, creating a significant amount of distance back to the hitting zone. You may experience trouble getting to the ball in time, especially when facing a pitcher who throws hard.

Wrapping your bat is also a common mistake. Wrapping means the angle of your bat cocks too far behind your head when you move to the launch position. If the bat were the hand of a clock, it would point to 12:00 when held straight up and down. The correct position (when viewed from behind the hitter) is for the bat to point to 11:00, maybe even 10:30. If it points to 10:00 or 9:30, you're wrapping your hands. Again, this creates too much distance for the barrel to get to the ball. Ease up on the wrist cock and you'll avoid wrapping the bat.

Separation

Because taking your stride and moving your hands back to the launch position happen at nearly the same time, many refer to it as separation. Your lower body and upper body move in separate directions. Although these movements travel in opposite directions, they are similar in that they're both subtle movements. They are not rushed or exaggerated. Separation combines two simple movements that put the hitter in a powerful position to hit the softball.

WEIGHT SHIFT

Hip rotation and weight shift are critical components of the swing. To hit the ball hard, and to hit it to all fields, you must rotate your hips and have some forward momentum moving into the ball when swinging the bat. Young hitters commonly fail to do this and as a result their hitting prowess suffers.

These elements of the swing can be developed only through time and repetition. It's not a quick and easy adjustment that is easily incorporated, but rather learned through continual training. As is often said, "Practice makes perfect."

Linear Movement to the Ball

You may have heard a coach or parent yell out to you, "keep your weight back," or "stay back on the ball." The reason you keep your weight back is so that you have something in reserve to go forward into the ball as it approaches the hitting zone. This forward movement is referred to as "linear movement." After the stride has planted and the hands have moved to the launch position, the hitter employs a minimal linear movement or "weight shift" toward the ball. This movement transfers energy into your forward swing.

The movement is not much more than a few inches forward. It's sometimes even difficult to detect by the blind eye. Exaggerating this movement (moving farther forward than necessary) can be detrimental to your swing.

To understand why this movement is important, try this simple experiment. Get into your batting stance. You won't need a bat for this exercise, but instead, hold a softball in your throwing hand. Because you're in your batting stance, carry more weight (approximately 60 percent) on your rear leg.

First, drop your arm and throw the ball as far as you can, but do not allow your weight to transfer forward onto your front leg. As your arm swings up and releases the ball, keep your weight on your back leg. As you release the ball, it will almost feel as if you're falling backward.

Next, throw a second ball as far as you can, but this time, allow your weight to transfer forward to a stiff front leg. You can throw the ball a lot farther, can't you? This is because you've put your entire body into your throw, not just your arm and shoulder. The same rule applies to hitting.

Any action in sports that involves striking an object requires some form of weight shift. A golfer hitting her tee shot, a tennis player smashing a forehand, and a volleyball player hitting an overhand serve are all acts that demonstrate the use and importance of weight shift.

Stiffen the Front Leg

Weight shift is important to hitting the ball with authority, but it has to be controlled. To do so, your front leg must stiffen to accept the momentum of your weight shift.

As the stride foot plants on the ground, the front leg is slightly bent and relaxed. Once you start shifting your weight forward to initiate the swing, the front leg must become rigid to control your forward movement. Bracing the front leg keeps your weight and balance over home plate.

Once the front leg is stiff, it acts like a post from which the hips can now rotate around. Think of a swinging gate. The post is stiff which allows the gate to swing open and close. If the post was unstable, the gate would be unable to move forcefully.

A Bent Front Leg

Failing to stiffen the front leg causes several problems. By keeping the knee bent, you'll be unable to stop your weight from moving forward. Your weight will carry outside your front leg, and you'll lose the strength of your lower body. The swing will appear as if you're reaching for the ball out in front of home plate and will be devoid of power.

As your weight shifts forward, your front leg must stiffen (as shown) to accept the weight transfer and allow your hips to forcefully rotate.

In addition, a bent front leg allows your head to move too far forward, making it very difficult to track the pitch. Any major head movement disrupts your sense of timing and distorts vision. Lastly, your hips will lack explosiveness because there is no firm post from which they can forcefully rotate. Little or no hip rotation slows down your bat speed and inhibits quickness. Inside pitches will be very difficult to handle.

HIP ROTATION

To utilize your major muscles (lower back, torso, buttocks, legs) when swinging the bat, you must rotate your hips. Hip rotation engages those parts of the body, adding power and speed to your hacks at the ball.

Before discussing the principles of hip rotation, understand one thing clearly: the upper and lower body must be thought of separately during the swing. If you're concentrating on explosive hip movement, focus on the lower body only. Disengage the lower half from your upper half. When you rotate your hips, you can not rotate your upper body (shoulders) along with them. This causes you to pull your front shoulder off the ball prematurely. The hips clear first and create a path for the hands to travel. If the hips and shoulders move simultaneously, you'll produce a defective swing.

The best way to describe hip rotation is to characterize the position of the hips before and after the swing. During the stance and stride, the hips are aligned with the pitcher. Much like the feet and shoulders, a straight line can be drawn along your waistline straight out to the pitcher's mound. After the swing is completed (and we'll assume the pitch is a strike down the middle), your belly button faces the pitcher.

How do you get to this position? Well, as your weight shifts forward, your back knee turns in towards the pitcher's mound. Your back foot pivots and heel is lifted up off the ground as you rotate your hips around. Some coaches tell their hitters to "fire the hips" or "spin on your back foot." This is in hopes of getting the hitter to rotate the hips quickly.

Hip rotation occurs after the stride foot is planted and before the hands begin the forward swing. The hips open a bit earlier and lead the hands through the hitting zone. Many hitters mistakenly allow the hips to trail the hands. This is incorrect. If they begin rotating after the hands move forward, power and bat speed are lost.

ADJUST THE HIPS TO THE PITCH

The hips rotate every time you swing the bat, but to what degree they rotate depends on the location of the pitch. The breakdown is very simple. On inside strikes, the hips fully rotate. Your belly button faces the area between shortstop and second base (assuming you're a right-handed hitter). On strikes down the middle, the hips rotate substantially, but

Notice the degree of hip rotation prior to contact. This increases bat speed and clears a path for the barrel to travel and meet the ball.

not completely. Your belly button faces the pitcher. On outside strikes, your hips rotate marginally. Your belly button faces the area between second base and the second base position (for right-handed batters).

Contact is made out in front of home plate on inside strikes. To get the barrel there in time, the hips must rotate quickly and completely. Hip rotation is extremely important to handling the inside strike. If they stay closed, you'll take one off the handle (get jammed).

Middle strikes are contacted at the top of home plate. The hips must fire, but not completely. If your hips rotate too far, your front shoulder will pull off the ball and your barrel will drop. Stay balanced and focus on hitting the ball back through the middle.

Outside strikes are always the most difficult to handle. This is due to two common faults. 1) The hitter does not allow the pitch to travel deep enough and contacts the ball out in front of home plate. 2) The hips rotate too far and pull the upper body away from the ball. The arms then extend prematurely to meet the ball and the barrel dips. If your body is moving one way and the ball is moving the other, it usually results in a weak hit.

Establishing comfort in adjusting the degree of hip rotation to pitch location is a gradual process. Start by hitting off of a batting tee. Set up the tee to hit middle strikes, inside strikes, and then outside strikes. Feel the difference in hip rotation as you work each pitch rotation.

Next, have someone stand behind a screen and flip you balls from the front (about 15 feet away). Ask them to vary the locations, starting with middle strikes, moving inside, and then outside. Again, feel the difference in hip rotation for each pitch location.

ADJUSTING THE HIPS AND POINT OF CONTACT TO THE PITCH

Pitch Location	Degree of Hip Rotation	Point of Contact
Inside Strikes	Full hip rotation	In front of home plate
Middle Strikes	Substantial hip rotation	Top of home plate
Outside Strikes	Minimal hip rotation	Middle of home plate

THE SWING

The correct pre-swing movements are of little value without a fundamentally sound swing. As Hall of Fame baseball player Tony Oliva once repeated, "It don't mean a thing if you ain't got that swing."

Each hitter's swing is unique, but there are some general guidelines that all should follow. The best hitters have short swings. That means the barrel of the bat moves from the launch position directly to the hitting zone. There are no wasted movements before firing the bat. Any additional movements will lengthen the swing and diminish bat speed. Long swings arrive to the hitting zone (and ball) too late. Diminished bat speed will limit your power and consistency in making solid contact.

Level Through the Hitting Zone

A proper swing is level through the hitting zone. Level swings afford the greatest chance of solid contact. To illustrate this, hold a bat out so it's parallel to the ground. In this position, the barrel of the bat has the broadest hitting surface for an incoming pitch. If you contact the ball perfectly in the middle, you'll hit a line drive. A ball hit just below the middle of the barrel will still produce a hard-hit ball. As you're holding the bat, dip the barrel slightly toward the ground. Because the ball is round you have now reduced the size of your hitting surface. It's possible to hit a ball square (although more difficult), but if the ball contacts the barrel just above middle, it's a pop-up or lazy fly ball to the outfield. A ball that catches the bat slightly below the middle will produce a chopper or weak ground ball. Keep the bat level to increase your chances of hitting a line drive.

From the launch position, the hands are pulled forward and down to the ball. Notice how the right arm is kept in, near the midsection. The hands are cocked and ready to fire the barrel. Extending that arm outward would produce a long swing.

The first movement of the forward swing is extremely significant. From the launch position, the hands initially move forward and down. The lead elbow inches out toward the pitcher's feet. This movement is important because it leads the barrel of the bat on a direct path toward the incoming pitch. Do not move your hands out away from your body or in towards your body. If your first movement with the hands is outward, you'll have a long swing and swing "around" the ball instead of "to" the ball.

The hitter is in great position at contact. The front foot is closed, and front leg stiff. Her hips have rotated, allowing her to generate bat speed and fire the barrel out in front of the plate. For consistent, solid contact, the bat stays level through the hitting zone and eyes are locked down on the ball.

This is called "casting" your hands, which manufactures a swing devoid of power and quickness. Moving your hands in toward your body corrupts your swing. The lead arm dominates the swing and the barrel will trail behind your hands. Hits will travel weakly to the opposite field. Start your hands forward and down to initiate a quick, punishing swing.

As the hips clear, the hands continue their path to the ball. The lead arm (bottom hand arm) guides the swing in its early stages. The knob of the bat should face the pitcher. During this time, the barrel of the bat remains tilted upward, above the ball. The top hand then begins to take over the swing as the pitch nears. It fires or propels the barrel of the bat forward through the hitting zone. At this point, the plane of the bat levels off, giving you the broadest hitting surface.

The hands and wrists fire the barrel into the ball. When contact is made, the hands are in the "palm-up, palm-down"

As the ball is hit, the hands should be in the palm-up, palm-down position. This means that the top-hand palm is facing up toward the sky, and the bottom-hand palm is facing down toward the ground.

position. This means the top hand faces up toward the sky and the bottom hand faces down toward the ground. The palm-up, palm-down position allows both hands to stay through the ball at contact. A com-

Coaches often tell hitters to "hit through the ball." This means that the hands explode through the ball, and roll over into the follow-through after contact.

To maintain bat speed and produce a powerful swing, follow through completely to finish the swing.

mon fault softball hitters commit is that they roll their top hand too quickly. This raises the barrel of the bat above the ball and produces ground balls to the pull side.

Remember that you don't want to simply "hit" the ball, you want to "drive" through the ball. Stay short to it and long through it.

FOLLOW-THROUGH

After contact is made and the bat begins ascending out of the hitting zone, break into your follow-through. Follow through every time you swing the bat. Cutting your swing short has an adverse effect on your forward swing. To stop your bat short of a full follow-through, you must slow your bat down prematurely. This is a subconscious effort, but indeed diminishes your bat speed and force into and through the softball. Complete the follow-through every time you swing the bat.

Where your swing finishes depends on several factors. Where your hands begin, personal swing path, and the location of the pitch all influence your follow-through. We suggest that you finish just over your shoulder. This promotes a level swing that ascends slightly once the bat leaves the hitting zone. By finishing lower than the rear shoulder, you'll run the risk of rolling your top hand too soon and cutting your swing short. Finishing too high might influence your swing to leave the hitting zone too quickly and promote a low-to-high swing path, or an uppercut.

HITTING ZONE VS. THE STRIKE ZONE

Now that you know the basic fundamentals of a good swing, you need to focus on *when* to take the bat off your shoulder. Good hitters become easy outs when they don't practice good plate discipline. To develop discipline, you must first learn the strike zone. The strike zone is the area over home plate where pitches are called a strike. Once you've learned the strike zone, take it a step farther and establish your own personal hitting zone. Your hitting zone is the area where you like your pitches best. Some hitters like them high, others low, some like them inside and others like pitches out over the plate. Time and experience, success and failure determine your hitting zone.

The Strike Zone

According to the Official Softball Rules Handbook, the defined strike zone is any pitch that crosses over home plate that is at or above the hitter's kneecaps and at or below her arm-pits. That is the defined strike zone. In reality, very few umpires call pitches above the belt a strike. It's important to know that pitches above the belt *can* be called a strike, but if the umpire is not calling it, let the pitch go for a ball. High strikes are difficult to hit and often result in swings and misses and pop-ups.

This brings us to a critical point. Just as girls have their own individual tastes in music or have a favorite dinner, umpires have their own personal strike zone. Some umpires have low strike zones (call low pitches strikes) and others have a high strike zone (call the high pitches strikes). Umpires' strike zones also differ horizontally. Some expand the strike zone and call pitches just off home plate strikes.

Others have tight strike zones and are apprehensive to call pitches on the corners strikes.

As a hitter, pay attention to any trends or patterns the umpire displays during the game. Use the information to your advantage. For example, if the umpire is not calling low strikes and the pitcher is serving up a steady diet of pitches down in the strike zone, let them pass. If the umpire continuously calls that pitch a ball, you'll hit ahead in the count all day. The pitcher will be forced to raise her pitches and throw them up around your thighs and belt—a fat pitch. By exhibiting patience, the umpire's personal strike zone can be beneficial to you.

Conversely, when an umpire has a large strike zone, be prepared to swing the bat, especially with two strikes. Many umpires, often found at the youth level, are trigger-happy and raise their hand to any pitch that is close to a strike. Factor this into your approach at the plate. Stay patient early in the count, but with two strikes, protect the plate (swing at anything close). The last thing you want is to be called out on strikes. To hit, you've got to swing the bat.

Never assume that you know the strike zone better than the umpire does. The umpire has 100 percent authority of what is being called balls and strikes for that day, so don't argue calls. Never in the history of softball has an umpire called a pitch a strike, listened to the batter's argument, and then decided to reverse his or her decision. It hasn't ever happened and never will happen. Disagreeing or becoming upset with umpires will only agitate them, which you'd rather not do. Conserve your thoughts and energy for the game. The umpire is the almighty judge.

Hitter's Counts

Swinging at strikes increases your chances of hitting the ball hard and getting on base. Having a good eye can also help you force the pitcher to serve you good strikes to hit—the kind that will enable you to send the outfielders scampering.

By not swinging at pitches outside of the strike zone, the count moves to your favor. These are called hitter's counts. When the count runs to 1-0, 2-0, 3-1, and even sometimes 3-2, the hitter has a distinct advantage over the pitcher. In these situations, the pitcher must throw a strike. When the pitcher *has* to throw a strike, she's less likely to nibble at the corners or try to fool you. She's going to come right at you. Would you rather try to hit a pitch on the outside corner, or one traveling down the middle? Being patient early in the count can often pay off later in the count.

When you work the pitcher into a hitter's count, be selectively aggressive. This means to attack the ball, but only if it's in a specific area. Approach the pitch assuming you're going to swing the bat and drive the ball, but if on tracking the ball you don't like its location, hold off and let it go. Remember that you're ahead in the count. Don't swing at a tough pitch unless you have two strikes.

The Hitting Zone

Every hitter has a personal hitting zone. Think back to when you were taking batting practice with your dad or friends and it was your turn. The pitcher called out, "Where do you like 'em?" You responded by holding your hand out in your favorite spot. In doing that, you described or defined the core location of your hitting zone. It's the spot where you like pitches best. When the pitcher puts one in that spot, you become a deadly hitter.

To define your hitting zone in greater detail, draw a rectangle that represents the strike zone. Think about where you like your pitches best and label those areas "hot." Then, label secondary locations where you handle the ball pretty well. Write down "warm" in these areas. Finally, jot down "cold" in the spots where you consistently have difficulty making solid contact. Anything located in the cold area is not a part of your hitting zone.

Now that you've defined your personal hitting zone, use that information for game action. When you get into hitter's counts, swing only at pitches that lie within your hitting zone. If you have the pitcher on the ropes and the count is 2-0 or 3-1, look for pitches in the "hot" zone. If the count is 1-1 or 2-1, look for pitches in the "hot" or "warm" zone. If the count is 1-2, 2-2, or 3-2, look for pitches in the "strike zone."

The hitting zone doesn't necessarily have to be part of the strike zone. Some hitters are labeled "bad-ball hitters" and like pitches in strange places. Ever see a hitter swing at a pitch up around her shoulders and watch her crush it for

Hitting becomes much easier if you swing only at pitches in the strike zone. Be aggressive on pitches in the strike zone. Be patient on pitches outside your hitting zone.

Each hitter possesses her own individual hitting zone. Some hitters like them high, others like them low, inside, or outside. If part of your hitting zone lies outside of the strike zone, you better make sure you hit it hard more often than not.

an extra base hit? If so, you witnessed a girl who has a hitting zone that expands outside of the strike zone. If you hit these pitches hard with consistency, it's part of your hitting zone.

The very best hitters work on expanding their hitting zone. The larger your hitting zone, the more difficult it is for a pitcher to get you out. Any areas outside of your hitting zone are areas of weakness. Work hard to shrink or eliminate these areas. It's fun to work on your strengths, but to improve at the plate, you must work on your weaknesses as well.

VISION

Vision is without question the most underestimated facet of hitting. Quite simply, you can't hit what you can't see. What your eyes see dictate whether you're going to swing the bat (pitch selection), when you're going to start your swing (timing), and where your swing path travels (pitch location). These three elements are critical to making consistent contact. Without any one of them, your chances of hitting the ball are slim. Without vision, the situation is hopeless.

Use Both Eyes at the Plate

Before discussing the various elements of vision, make sure you look out at the pitcher with both eyes. Do not turn your head inward and peer out with just one eye. Your vision skills improve tremendously by using both eyes.

Closing the shoulders in your stance often causes the mistake of using one eye. Instead of positioning your shoulder blades so they are aligned with the pitcher, you coil the front shoulder inward. When this happens, the head turns as well and both eyes will not face the pitcher. Don't be shy. Turn your head and face the pitcher.

Soft Center/Hard Focus

Where do I look before the pitcher starts her windup? Should I keep my eye on the ball the entire time the pitcher holds the ball? Do I pick up the ball after it's released? These are all good questions that must be addressed. They all can be answered by simply understanding the functions of soft center and hard focus.

A soft center is where your eyes should look before the pitcher begins her windup. It's a soft, relaxed gaze into a general area. The pitcher's jersey is a good area to target your soft center. The pitcher's cap, her face, or even center field works as well. Find an area that is around the pitcher, but not something too small or distinctive. Focusing on something too specific forces your eyes to work too hard, which may tire them out before the pitch is even released.

Keep your eyes in this general area throughout the pitcher's windup. Once her arm swings down and toward the release, it's time to switch to your hard focus. The hard focus is a concentrated stare on the pitcher's release point. Just before the pitcher releases the ball, your eyes must be locked on that area. To pick up the pitch location, spin, and speed, track the ball as soon as it leaves the pitcher's hand.

The transition from soft center to hard focus is extremely important. If it occurs too early, your eyes will tire and may lose focus or even blink as the pitch is en route. If it happens too late, you won't pick up the ball in time and it will be past you and in the catcher's glove before

Track each pitch with both eyes. It improves your vision and concentration.

At this point in the pitcher's delivery, your eyes shift to hard focus and lock onto the release point. Picking up the release too late makes it difficult to track the pitch.

you can even get the bat off your shoulder.

Picking Up the Pitcher's Release Point

In order for your eyes to quickly move to the pitcher's release point, determine the location of her release point. Most pitchers' release point will be right off their throwing side hip, but some will vary vertically. The length of a girl's arms, legs, how much she flexes her post leg, the type of pitch she's throwing, and the length of her stride all influence the height where pitchers release the ball.

To determine the pitcher's release point before your at bat, watch her warm up in the bullpen or while you're standing in the on-deck circle. Be prepared with this information before your at bat. Don't allow a perfect strike to pass by just because you were getting a feel for where she releases the ball.

FAULTS AND FIXES

Even though you're now well-versed in the art and science of hitting a softball, you will experience your share of struggles. Even the very best hitters experience slumps throughout a season. Executing the stance, pre-swing movements, swing, and follow-through without some type of mechanical breakdown every now and then is unlikely. It's the nature of the sport.

Making outs are as much a part of the game as is the national anthem. You're going to make outs and must learn to handle that ingredient of the game with class and maturity. It's essential to your progression as a hitter, however, to evaluate your outs. Don't simply grow frustrated. Pay attention to what type of outs you're making. If there is an obvious pattern, you can pinpoint the mechanical flaw. Are you constantly popping up to the infield? Are you hitting weak grounders to the pull side? Does it seem as if you're fooled on every pitch? By discovering a specific trend in your failures, you can determine the cause of your struggles.

WHEN A SLUMP IS NOT A SLUMP

Batting slumps are part of softball, but it's important to understand what is a slump and what is not. Too often, batting average and statistics are heavily scrutinized. Players feel that if they don't get a hit, they're doing something wrong. That is not the case.

With a pitcher throwing a variety of pitches to several locations, hitting the softball hard can be an arduous task. Factor in that there are nine defensive players stationed with gloves to get you out, and you quickly realize that accumulating hits is no guarantee even if you hit the ball hard.

As long as you're hitting the ball solid, don't worry about your statistics. If you hit a line drive right at the shortstop, you've done all you can do. Don't fret that your batting average has suffered. Go get them the next time. The ball bounces crazy ways and there are times when luck is simply not on your side. Don't create a slump in your mind if it's not warranted. Soon enough, the breaks will turn in your favor.

There are numerous errors in the swing that produce fruitless results. They develop in the stance, pre-swing movements, swing, and mental approach. Some swing faults, however, arise more often than others. If you're struggling at the plate, review the list of the 10 most common faults hitters make (see below). You might come across one that pertains to you. By identifying your swing fault, you can quickly put yourself back on the path to recovery.

First, read the description of the fault and why it's problematic. Then, review the poor game results that become all too familiar when guilty of the particular fault. Finally, follow the corrective action to eliminate the recurring mistake.

Poor Balance in the Stance

Why it's a problem. Without balance, you have no foundation from which to generate a controlled, powerful swing. It's very difficult to incorporate your lower body into the swing without balance, so you're swinging predominantly with your arms and wrists. Have you ever tried to throw off-balance or shoot a basketball from an unbalanced position? For starters, you have less control and secondly, you have less strength behind the action.

Also, an unsteady foundation has a rippling effect all the way to the top. Head movement will occur making it tough to track the incoming pitch. You'll experience problems determining balls and strikes, and identifying the type of pitch.

Game results. Swinging through pitches, chasing pitches out of the strike zone, weakly hit balls, poor bat speed.

The corrective action. Proper balance is accomplished by setting yourself in an athletic position. Spread your feet slightly farther than shoulder-width apart and stand on the balls of your feet. Do not allow yourself to rock back on your heels or forward onto your toes. Minimize the movement you have in your stance and pre-swing, but flex at the knees.

Take a relaxed, controlled swing. Swinging too hard, or exerting too much effort usually throws a hitter off balance. The swing should be short and quick, not long and hard.

Stepping in the Bucket

Why it's a problem. Stepping away from home plate (toward the pull-side of the field) carries the energy of your swing away from the ball. This drains you of power. The object is to step toward the pitcher, and direct your energy to and through the softball.

Stepping in the bucket diminishes plate coverage. You'll be unable to make solid contact with pitches on the outer half and outside corner of the plate. You'll become a one-dimensional hitter who can only handle pitches on the inner portion of the strike zone.

Lastly, as your stride moves open, your hips open up prematurely. The explosive hip torque generated from your torso and legs is minimized. Instead of firing the hips 90 degrees, you'll only fire them 60 degrees, which generates less power.

Game results. Difficulty hitting pitches on the outer half of the strike zone, ground balls to the pull-side of the infield come in bunches, lazy fly balls to the opposite field, less power.

The corrective action. To stop this particularly bad habit, train yourself to stride square to the pitcher. Repeat drills off of the batting tee and soft toss and focus exclusively on the direction of your stride. Next, take batting practice with the pitcher throwing from a shortened distance. While taking swings, place a bat on the ground just off your front foot's heel. The bat should point out toward center field. If you stride away from home plate, you'll step on the bat. Continue to use the bat on the ground during batting practice for at least a week. If after a week your stride is square on every pitch, remove the bat.

Drifting

Why it's a problem. Drifting means that as you're taking your stride, your weight shifts forward onto your front leg. This causes numerous problems. You'll have no energy (or weight) stored on your rear leg to explode into the ball as you swing the bat. Your front leg will be bent, which limits your hip rotation. Lastly, as your weight moves forward, your head moves forward. Any exaggerated movement forward with the head and eyes make it difficult to pick up the pitch. In addition, a 50 mile-per-hour fastball will appear as if it's traveling 55 miles per hour.

Game results. Swing is late, chasing pitches out of the strike zone, difficulty handling inside strikes, swings and misses, trouble with off-speed pitches.

The corrective action. Drifting occurs when hitters are overanxious and don't trust their bat speed. They tend to "go to" the pitch instead of sitting back and allowing it to come to them. First, take some strides on some sort of incline to get a feel for what it's like to keep your weight back as you stride. A pitcher's mound on a baseball field works well. Next, stand up at the plate with a pitcher throwing, but don't swing. Focus only on taking a soft stride and keeping your hands back. After 20 to 25 pitches, add your swing but hit balls only to the opposite field. This forces you to let the ball get to you.

Dropping the Rear Shoulder

Why it's a problem. Once the rear shoulder drops, you're in big trouble. Your swing path ascends through the hitting zone rather than traveling on a level path. When the barrel travels upward at the ball, it can easily catch the bottom of the ball (resulting in a pop-up) or the top of the ball (resulting in a chopper). Either way, you have a slim chance of hitting a line drive. Also, dropping the rear shoulder means the hands move down and back instead of forward and down. This lengthens your swing and slows your bat speed.

Game results. Pop-ups and lazy fly balls, top-spin ground balls and choppers, swings and misses, hitting balls below the barrel.

The corrective action. Stand approximately 15 feet away from a batting cage net. Place a hat on the ground just in front of the net straight ahead of you. With a partner feeding you a soft toss, attempt to hit balls at the hat. This forces your hands (and shoulder) to stay above the ball. Continue this drill each day for a week so the notion of dropping your rear shoulder is eliminated from your muscle memory.

Overswinging

Why it's a problem. Hitters overswing simply because they try to hit the ball too hard or too far. By doing this, you actually diminish bat speed and reduce power. In addition, you'll be late to pitches and hit the ball below the barrel of the bat (near the handle).

The reason these symptoms occur is because tension infiltrates the swing. By exerting too much effort, the muscles contract and you lose fluidity. The hands rush to the ball and the barrel trails behind.

A few other faults often arise when the hitter overswings as well. The front shoulder commonly pulls off the ball prematurely, creating a swing that moves away from the pitch and covers only the inside of the strike zone. Balance is lost, reducing power and bat control. Also, the head moves off the pitch and limits your ability to track the ball.

Game results. Fly balls to the opposite field, late on pitches, getting jammed, swings and misses, reduced power.

The corrective action. The way to combat overswinging is to relax and trust your abilities. Deep breathing and positive visualization are two methods of relaxation. You must train yourself to understand that less is more, meaning that by exerting a little less effort, you'll produce better bat speed. A quicker bat produces hits that leave the bat faster and travel farther. Relax and look to simply make solid contact.

Cutting the Swing Short

Why it's a problem. By stopping the swing short of a full follow-through, you're losing power and bat speed. To finish prematurely, you actually have to start slowing down your swing before you even make contact with the ball. Think about throwing a softball for distance. If you stop your throwing motion early and fail to follow through, you won't be able to throw the ball as far. The same principle applies when swinging the bat.

Game results. Failure to hit balls hard off the bat, balls constantly hit to the pull-side from rolling the top hand too soon, indecisive swings.

The corrective action. To execute a proper follow-through, the hitter must first gain a sense for what a proper follow-through feels like. The hitter should take dry swings and focus solely on completing the swing. Take aggressive swings (100 percent) so a full follow-through will transpire without additional effort. Lastly, take batting practice off of short toss and attempt to hit line drives back through the middle. This will keep your hands through the ball and stop you from rolling the wrists prematurely and cutting off the swing.

Premature Weight Shift

Why it's a problem. A hitter is guilty of premature weight shift when she moves her weight forward with the stride. Weight shift occurs with the swing, not the stride. Shifting the weight forward too early causes several problems. Your head moves forward, which makes it difficult to track the pitch. Moving toward the pitch slows your bat down because you'll be unable to forcefully rotate your hips. With that, you'll swing the bat with just your arms, failing to incorporate the power generated by your lower body.

This swing fault commonly occurs because hitters are overanxious. They want to "go to" the pitch instead of staying back and letting the pitch come to them.

Game results. Weak ground balls, weak fly balls, swinging on pitches out of the strike zone, late on fastballs.

The corrective action. You must train yourself to keep your weight back. To do so, have a friend or teammate throw pitches and simply take your stride. Focus on keeping your weight back. Do not swing the bat or worry about hitting the ball, just take your stride, and watch the pitch all the way in. This gives you a feel for staying back and also improves your timing. Watching the pitch in its entirety slows things down and makes you less anxious.

After 20–25 pitches, allow yourself to swing the bat. Hit each pitch to the opposite field. Hitting to the opposite field forces you to let the ball get deep in the hitting zone and keeps your weight back.

Improper Grip

Why it's a problem. Much like the stance, the grip is a basic foundation of your swing. Holding the bat improperly can ruin your swing. There are several mistakes a hitter can make when gripping a bat. You could hold the bat down in your palms, allow space between your hands, align your knuckles incorrectly, or grip the bat too tight. These problems lead to reduced power, bat speed, and bat control.

Game results. Hitting ground balls to the pull-side, hitting top-spin line drives, late on fastballs, unable to handle pitches on the outside part of the plate.

The corrective action. The only way to correct the grip is to go through a checklist to pinpoint your problem. Are you holding the bat in your fingers? Are your middle knuckles aligned? Is your grip free of tension? If you've answered "no" to any of these questions, make the proper adjustment immediately.

No Hip Rotation

Why it's a problem. Without hip rotation, you won't get the bat around quickly enough or with enough force to hit the ball solid. You'll struggle especially with pitches on the inside part of the plate.

The hips generate bat speed and clear a path for the hands to move freely into the hitting zone. Dormant hips force the hands to move around the torso and produce a swing that is "all arms." When the hips do not rotate open, inside strikes become difficult to handle. The only way to get the barrel of the bat on the ball is to sling the bat way out in front of home plate. As a result, your outfield hits will not carry. They'll hook or dip from top-spin, and frequently find foul territory.

Game results. Poor bat speed, little or no power, balls hit in the air will sink or hook, inside strikes hit below the barrel (jammed).

The corrective action. The hips must be incorporated into each swing. Without a bat, take your stride and rotate your hips so your belly button faces the pitcher (upon completion). Next, place a bat behind your back and practice rotating your hips with force. Finally, have someone flip you balls to the inside corner. Work on firing your hips and hitting the ball square to the pull-side.

Lack of Confidence

Why it's a problem. Perhaps the most detrimental fault of the group, lack of confidence can destroy a hitter's performance and ability to produce. An insecure mind makes you timid at the plate, adversely affects your vision, causes indecisiveness, and creates tension. You must believe in yourself to experience success. If you don't, you'll fail regularly.

Game results. Called strike threes, constantly hitting behind in the count, swinging at pitches out of the strike zone, weak and conservative swings (check swings).

The corrective action. The best way to gain confidence is to accumulate some hits, however, that's much easier said than done. Since you can't just decide to get hits, do the next best thing. Take extra batting practice to work on your swing. Extra swings can iron out any mechanical flaws, but also put you in a more positive frame of mind. If you enter the game feeling well prepared, you'll eliminate feelings of insecurity and replace them with self-assurance.

DRILLS

Tee Work

There is no better instrument to refine your hitting mechanics than a batting tee. Because the ball sits on the batting tee, it eliminates factors such as timing and pitch location so you can focus solely on swing mechanics.

Position the tee as if you were hitting a pitch down the middle. (The stem of the tee should be set near the top of home plate.) Hit balls into a net directly in front of you. Your goal is to hit every ball on a straight line up the middle. If your hits travel above, below, or to the left or right of that middle mark, make the proper adjustments to your swing. (For example, if you hit the ball above your mark, you're probably uppercutting. Keep your rear shoulder up and level off your swing.)

To simulate inside and outside strikes, make the following adjustments to the tee's positioning. The proper point of contact for inside strikes lies in front of home plate, so move the tee forward and closer to you. The proper point of contact for outside strikes is near the middle of home plate, so move the tee back and away from you. Make sure the tee is set up in these positions when practicing specific pitch locations.

For your first round, hit 15 strikes down the middle. Next, hit 10 outside strikes followed by 10 inside strikes. Finish up with 10 strikes down the middle.

Note: During your next session, raise and lower the tee to simulate high and low strikes.

Long Tee

Set up a tee on home plate so you're hitting the length of a batting cage. The goal of this drill is to hit line drives into the back net of the cage. The tee is positioned as if the pitch is a strike down the middle. Take game-speed swings with effort to hit line drives back through the middle.

If your hits carry into the back net on a line, you've accomplished your goal. Some hits, however, may travel to the pull-side, the opposite field, straight into the ground, or up into the top of the cage. If this happens, make the appropriate adjustment to your swing. For example, if your hits continuously travel to the pull-side, ease up with your top hand and stay through the ball with two hands. Feel your lead arm play a more significant role in the swing.

Hitting off of a tee helps refine your mechanics, but the long tee drill enables you to observe your ball flight. This helps you discover swing faults.

Regular soft toss requires a coach to kneel and toss balls underhand from a 45 degree angle. Focus on your mechanics as you hit balls into a net or screen.

Soft Toss

With a tosser flipping balls at you from a 45 degree angle, take your stride and hit balls into a net. The tosser must first bring her arm back and then forward to flip the ball so you can time the tosses. The ball is thrown toward the front hip approximately belt-high. It

On pitches high in the strike zone, raise your hands to keep the barrel above the ball. Don't swing up, but rather swing level at the pitch. On balls low in the strike zone, lower your body with your legs and keep the bat on a level swing plane.

should travel on a straight line (no arc). This drill can help establish proper mechanics, rhythm, and hand-to-eye coordination. Use it to get loose before a game or practice.

Hi-Low

Stationed in the same position as a regular soft toss, the tosser flips balls both high and low in the strike zone. As she swings her arm forward, the tosser should say "Hi" or "Low". This gives the hitter enough time to adjust her swing to the pitch location.

On high tosses, focus on raising your hands to the height of the ball and swing the bat on a level plane. Don't swing up at the ball (uppercut) to make contact. For low strikes, use your legs to lower your body to the pitch. This brings the eyes closer to the ball and enables the bat to get on a level plane. Do not drop the barrel of the bat to the ball. This is a poor technique that produces pop-ups and foul balls. Use your legs to lower your body.

Quick Toss

Stationed in the soft-toss position, the tosser says "stride" and the hitter takes her stride. The tosser then fires a crisp toss in toward the hitter's front hip. The hitter's goal is to do whatever it takes to put the barrel of the bat on the ball. This is a difficult drill that requires a short swing and quick hands. The tosser must challenge the hitter with each flip. If the hitter is finding the ball with the barrel easily, increase the speed of the toss.

Front Toss

To set up this drill, you'll need a screen to protect the tosser. Standing approximately 15 feet in front of the batter, the tosser underhand tosses balls to the hitter and quickly moves behind the screen (for protection). Because a toss from this direction simulates game action, it's helpful to the hitter. Even more important, the tosser can easily vary the location of her tosses. She can throw them high, low, inside, or outside. The hitter must assess the location of the toss and adjust her mechanics accordingly.

This drill is very useful when a particular pitch location is giving you trouble. For example, if you find the low and inside strike is a weakness, request that the tosser throw continuously to that spot. By training yourself to hit pitches in this location, you'll eliminate that weakness and expand your hitting zone.

One-Handed Hacker

To better understand the role each arm has in the swing, break things down in this top-hand, bottom-hand drill.

First, work the top hand. Take the bottom hand off of the bat and choke up with the top hand. Choke all the way up to the top of the grip. Hold your bottom hand (left hand if you're right-handed) in toward your midsection. From the standard soft-toss position, the tosser flips balls to you. Fire the bat directly to the ball, hitting them into the net in front of you. Concentrate on using your hand, wrist, and forearm to provide the punch, not the shoulder.

Next, work the bottom hand. Take the top hand off of the bat and choke up with the bottom hand. Choke all the way up to the top of the grip. Hold your top hand (right hand if you're right-handed) in toward your midsection. Repeat the same exercise as described above, using your hand, wrist, and forearm to fire the barrel. This variation of the drill is commonly more difficult than the top hand, so be patient.

This drill helps the hitter understand the role each arm contributes to the swing. Make sure the swing travels down to the ball and then levels off. Don't allow the bat to dip and then come up at the ball, which will produce a ball hit in the air. Keep the barrel on a level plane.

Isolating the top and bottom hand allows the hitter to feel the function of each in the swing. The hitter should focus on keeping the bat level and using her hand, wrist, and forearm to propel the barrel of the bat forward. Make sure you choke up four or five inches.

The Happy Gilmore Drill

Ever seen the movie *Happy Gilmore* starring Adam Sandler? In that movie, Adam Sandler plays a former hockey player who finds he can hit a golf ball unprecedented distances by using a unique approach. He stands a few steps behind the ball and walks up to it (instead of standing over it). Without breaking stride, he takes his final step and whacks the ball a prodigious distance. This drill is very similar.

Set a softball on a batting tee. Take three or four steps back away from your stance position. Take slow steps up to the tee. Stride and then swing in one continuous motion. Your natural instincts will guide you in pushing your hands back to your rear shoulder—the power position—before swinging the bat. Take a healthy cut and drive the ball with power.

This drill helps the hitter feel two important elements of the swing. 1) The hitter will move her hands back to the power position—the position from which the hitter starts the forward swing. 2) The hitter will feel her weight shift to and through the softball. Her forward momentum (built up from her approach to the tee) should continue forward with the swing.

GAMES

Opposite Field Fever

With a coach or teammate throwing batting practice, each player hits the balls with the intention of hitting the ball to the opposite field side of second base. Keep track of how many balls out of 10 you successfully hit to the opposite field. Whoever tallies the most successful hits win. Pop-ups or ground balls that do not reach the outfield grass don't count toward your score.

Three-peat

In a batting cage, set up the L-screen for the front toss drill. (To do this, place the straight side of the screen on your throwing side.) This game trains the hitter to hit to all fields. The hitter must hit three consecutive line drives to opposite field, three through the middle, and three to the pull-side. Here's how the game works.

The tosser flips the ball to the outside part of the plate first. The hitter attempts to hit a line drive into the opposite-field side of the cage. She must hit three consecutive line drives in order to move onto middle hits. If the batted ball hits the top of the cage net, the ground, or to the middle or pull-side areas, the hitter must start over.

After she hits three straight to the opposite field net, she moves onto the middle. She must hit three straight balls into the L-screen or the back of the cage to move onto pull-side hits. If she fails to hit a line drive up the middle, she must begin the middle stage over again. (You do not, however, fall all the way back to the opposite-field hits.) This process is repeated again for pull-side hits.

The tosser must do her best to flip balls to the outside corner for opposite-field hits, down the middle for central hits, and to the inside corner for pull-side hits. If the hitter decides to take a pitch (not swing) because of poor location, she is not to be penalized.

The batter is hoping to get through all three stages using the least amount of swings. The best possible score is nine swings. The lowest number of swings it takes a player to complete all three stages wins the game.

Indian Softball

This is a fun game the whole team can play. Players are divided into two groups. One team plays defense, while the other hits.

Each player on the offensive team hits once. The object is to hit the ball and touch as many bases as possible. Each bag touched while circling the bases is worth a point.

The defense must field the ball, get all their players behind the fielded ball in a single-file line, and pass the ball between their legs. The last person in line throws the ball in to the pitcher on the mound. Once the pitcher catches the ball, the runner's turn is over.

The key to this game is bat control. If the first batter hits the ball to left field, the entire defense must run over to left field to form their line. Once they throw the ball into the pitcher's mound, the pitcher is instructed to immediately throw to the next batter. If the batter has enough savvy with the stick to hit the ball to right field, the entire team has to run all the way to right field. This gives the hitter more time to circle the bases.

Once everyone on the offensive team hits, the teams switch and the defense gets their turn at the plate. The team that accumulates the most combined points wins the game. The losing team must perform a conditioning exercise of the coach's choice.

Impenetrable defense can make the difference between a good team and a championship team.

3

FUNDAMENTALS OF DEFENSE

One of the most widely accepted softball axioms is that "you win with pitching and defense." Notice the inclusion of defense—catching and throwing—because great pitching can be nullified by poor defense. It's very simple: you can't be a consistent winner if you don't know how to catch and throw the ball effectively.

Sure, catching and throwing the ball are the skills you learned first, probably in the backyard with mom and dad. As simple as these tasks may seem, many games are won and lost because of a player's inability to catch or throw, so you should work on your catching and throwing every day.

Remember, few things in softball are more exciting than a great fielding gem (or as they call it on SportsCenter, a "Web Gem"). Whether it's a shortstop ranging into the hole between short and third to turn a sure base hit into an out, or an outfielder making a powerful throw to the plate to nail an opposing runner attempting to score, great defensive play is electric. Hitting may be more glamorous, but the coaches know that more games are won by solid defense.

THROWING THE BALL

The key to proper throwing is good mechanics—getting your arms, legs, and torso to work together.

"Proper mechanics enables the player to throw the ball with speed and with the best control possible," says Lisa Fernandez, who has pitched and played third base for the 1996 and 2000 Gold Medal

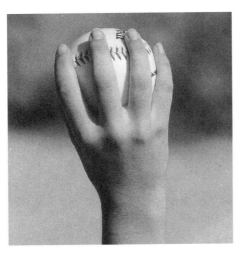

This photo illustrates the basic four-seam grip. Hold the ball in your fingers, not in the palm of your hand.

Point your lead arm toward the target as you bring the ball back. Notice how her hand remains on top of the ball during her backswing.

Olympic Teams. "Proper mechanics also improves endurance and reduces the chance for injury."

Games are often won and lost due to poor throwing. Errors occur because of a poor grip, a bad exchange when transferring the ball from the glove into the throwing hand, or rushing to throw before the ball is properly positioned in the fingers of the throwing hand. (*see photo*)

GRIPPING THE BALL

You should grip the ball across the seams, or laces, with two, three, or four fingers, depending on your age and hand size. Place your thumb and pinkie finger along opposite sides of the ball for support and stability. This is called the "four-seam" grip, and it enables you to put backspin on the ball. This is the best spin for creating carry, or distance.

As much as you can, hold the ball with your fingers, not with the palm of your hand. Your fingers give you more control and power. Too much palm on the ball increases friction and inhibits wrist action, thereby decreasing the speed you are able to impart on your throws. Practice your grip every day, so that it becomes second-nature during the game.

STEP AND FIRE

Once you've gripped the ball, it's time to remove it from the glove and throw it toward your target. Take the ball out of the glove and move your hand back and up, until your elbow is approximately at shoulder-height. This back-swing should be relatively short, nothing more than a quick loop back and up. Your hand should be positioned so that the upper and lower parts of your arm form a right angle at your elbow. At the same time, step toward your target with your left foot (if you are a right-handed thrower) and point your glove-arm toward toward the target, while rotating your shoulders and hips until they are in a direct line to your target. Push your weight back on the ball-side foot.

As you start your throw, the ball will travel forward past your ear, with the fingers on top of the ball and the palm down. The palm must be in this position to allow you to snap your wrist as you release the ball. As your arm accelerates into the throw, pivot on the ball of your back foot and shift your weight from your back foot to your front. As you release the throw, feel the ball rotate off your fingertips. At the same time, you should pull your lead arm into your chest, near your heart, as you shift your weight forward.

Step directly toward the target when throwing the ball. Your weight shifts forward onto a stiff front leg as the ball is released out in front of your body.

FOLLOW THROUGH

Remember, you must finish the throw by following through. Don't stop your arm after the ball has left your hand. You want to fully extend your arm toward the target. A good fol-

Whether it's from third to first or home to second, follow through every time you throw the ball.

low-through should allow your throwing hand to finish across your body outside of the opposite leg, between your knee and shin.

Many young players tend to throw the ball with an arc that is too high, especially from the outfield. Try to throw the ball straight, low, and hard. Don't increase the distance at which you play catch.

CATCHING A THROW

Catching a thrown ball is one of the most basic skills in the game, so it's surprising that so many players don't do it right. The key to catching a throw is to be prepared, with your body in the ideal position and your mind focused on the task at hand.

FINDING THE RIGHT GLOVE

All gloves are not created equal. For example, outfielders and pitchers generally use larger gloves than infielders, and catchers and first basemen use gloves specially designed for those positions.

First, find a glove that fits your hand. Make sure that it's not so big that you can't control it. Make sure that it's easy for you to get the ball out of the glove quickly. And it's important to remember that you are shopping for a *softball glove,* not a baseball glove. They are not the same. Softball gloves have a larger pocket (catching area) and longer fingers.

After you find a glove you like, you'll need to break it in. The best way to break a glove in is to soften the pocket of the glove by applying glove oil or vaseline to the surface. To help form the pocket, place a softball inside the glove—in the exact center of the pocket—then hold the ball in position by tying the glove around the ball with a piece of shoelace. After the pocket has been formed, play catch regularly. Don't use the glove in a game situation until it is completely broken in.

READY AND WAITING

To receive a throw, get your body behind the ball, with your glove in front of your body and with the pocket open to receive the ball. Your arms should be extended, but with some flexion in your elbows. Your knees should be slightly flexed, with your head up and your eyes fixed on the ball. As the ball nears, adjust your glove according to the direction of the throw. For example, if it is a low throw, you must turn the fingers of your glove down, so that the pocket faces up, or if the throw is opposite your glove-side, you must reach across your body with the fingers of your glove "pointing" at the ball.

Whenever possible, catch the ball out away from you, in the center of your body, and with your stride foot ahead of your pivot foot. This enables you to see the ball all the way into your glove, and it makes it

When receiving the ball, stand with your feet shoulder-width apart and hold your glove out in front of you, giving your teammate a target.

Whenever possible, catch the ball with two hands. It's the surest way to receive the ball.

easier to transfer the ball into your throwing hand. Your foot position will save you time as you prepare to throw the ball. If the throw is off-center or wild, quickly move your feet to get into better position.

GET IT OUT QUICKLY

After a catch, the ball should spend as little time as possible in your glove. Remember, while you're holding the ball in your glove, the base runners are still moving.

As soon as the ball strikes your glove, move quickly to secure it with your throwing hand. This will keep the ball from popping out of your glove. Next, quickly grip the ball, remove it from your glove, and throw it to your target. Transferring the ball quickly from glove to hand is particularly important during relay plays and when executing double plays.

FIELDING GROUND BALLS

In softball, batters hit far more ground balls than fly balls, so all defensive positions, infield and outfield alike, must be proficient at fielding ground balls. You should practice fielding ground balls every day.

Think of it this way: ground balls are a routine part of the game. If you aren't good at a routine part of the game, how will the coach find a place to play you?

INFIELD GROUND BALLS
To field an infield ground ball, or "grounder," requires confidence and courage. You must move your body directly in front of the ball, without fear, and come to a momentary stop while making the catch. If you field the ball while running (which you sometimes must do), both catching and then throwing the ball are more difficult.

GET READY
The basic position of an infielder is a semi-crouch: you are facing the batter, knees bent, your arms in front of your body, and your weight forward on the balls of your feet. Keep your glove in front of you, about six inches away from the ground, always ready for the ball. Some players like to take a step as the pitch is being delivered, and then immediately get into the ready position. This is a great way to get ready for action, since it ensures that your weight is forward and your body is ready to move.

When the ball is hit, immediately move toward it as quickly as you can. Move quickly but stay under control. Do not charge wildly at the ball. When you reach the point of intercepting the ball, come to a momentary stop, square your shoulders to the ball, and stay low. Keep your hands down and well out in front of your body, with the thumbs pointing out. It's easier to raise your hands to catch a ball than it is to lower them.

Set up to field the ball in the middle of your body. Flex your knees and lower your rear end. As the ball approaches, extend both hands to field the ball out in front of your feet.

MAKING THE PLAY
To make the play, keep your feet apart for good balance and reach out for the ball. Use both hands and extend them to meet the ball well out in front of your body. Imagine that your feet and hands form the points of an equilateral triangle. A line drawn between the tips of your feet form the base, and your outstretched hands form the top of the triangle.

Keeping the glove low to the ground when approaching a grounder will make it less likely that the ball will go through your legs. Keep your eyes on the ball. As the ball enters the glove, remember to "give" with the ball to absorb its impact. Next, move your throwing hand to cover the ball. Now move both hands toward the starting point of your throw, with your throwing hand gripping the ball.

If you are unable to field the ball cleanly, do what you can to keep it in front of you. Block it with your body. Always dive at balls out of your normal reach. Your primary object is to keep the ball in the infield. Be aggressive.

When fielding a backhand, your final step is a crossover step with your glove-side foot. Bend at the knees, reach across your body, and lock the ball into your glove.

ON THE MOVE

Many times the ball is hit to your side. If it's hit slightly to one side, take a few short sliding steps to bring your body behind the ball. When the ball is hit far off to your side, begin sprinting to the ball with a crossover step. When a ball is hit to your right, for example, pivot on the balls of your feet and cross your left foot over your right, keeping your glove low to the ground. This turns your body to the side of the ball, and you can run to the point where you wish to intercept the ball. Again, if you have time, make sure you square your body to the ball when making the catch.

Sometimes the ball is hit so that it is impossible for you to get your body in front of it. If this happens to your throwing-arm side, you have to do what is called "backhanding" the ball. Here's how to do it:

- Use a crossover step to get your body sideways to the ball.
- Sprint to where you will intercept the ball.
- Your final step should be a crossover step as you reach across your body with the glove hand.
- As you reach, turn your glove over so the fingers are pointed downward.
- Keep the glove open and then close it quickly once the ball enters the pocket.

At times, balls hit hard to your left must be fielded on the run. Reach down and field the ball off your left foot.

With runners on base, field ground balls in the outfield like an infielder. Keep your body in front of the ball in case it takes an unpredictable bounce.

Use this same approach when balls are hit to your glove-hand side, except cross over with your throwing-side foot to turn your body sideways. Sprint to the ball. Your final step is with your glove-side foot. You should field the ball, just off your glove-side foot, your knees and waist bent.

Outfield Ground Balls

The most important thing for an outfielder to remember when fielding a ground ball: *You are the last line of defense. Anything that gets past you is big trouble for the team.*

Your body position is slightly different from an infielder's, because you must always be ready to sprint to a ball. Stand upright, with your knees slightly bent, and hold your glove out waist-high. As you run to the ball, don't keep the glove out in front, but pump your arms as if you were running in a race. As you get closer to the ball, slow down and get your body under control. Make sure your body is in front of the ball, then field the ball like an infielder, adjusting your technique according to the game situation.

SITUATION 1—PLAY IT COOL

If the ball is traveling slowly and with no runners on base, drop to one knee to ensure the ball doesn't get by you. When you drop to one knee, drop to the knee on your throwing side. Keep your glove on the ground so the ball can't roll through your legs, and you should field the ball in the center of your body.

SITUATION 2—PICK UP THE PACE

If the ball is hit hard and is traveling at high speed, field it like you would in the infield. This gives you better mobility, especially if the ball takes a bad hop and happens to get past you. You will also be in a better position to throw the ball to your target.

SITUATION 3—DO OR DIE

The do-or-die method is used when you have to field the ball on the run and release a throw quickly. This is a risky maneuver, and the time to use this technique is when the game is on the line and a base runner is attempting to score or advance into scoring position.

Once the ball is hit, sprint to it and scoop it up on the run. If possible, field the ball on your glove side; it's easier. Try to step with the glove side foot as you field the ball, as it will save time on your throw. If you are right-handed, step with your left foot as you field the ball. Then step with your right foot to stand up and grip the ball, and take a step with your left foot as you throw the ball. This technique saves you time when making the catch and throw, time that can prevent a base runner from scoring.

With no one on base, drop to one knee to make sure the ball stays in front of you. Field the ball with two hands in the middle of your body.

In a run-scoring situation, field the ball on the run. Field it out in front of you, just off your glove-side foot.

FLY BALLS

Playing the outfield requires many skills. Among them are speed and a strong, accurate throwing arm, both tangible skills that are easy to spot in a player. But one of the most important skills an outfielder must possess is not so easy to identify. It's the ability to judge, track, and catch fly balls.

ANTICIPATING AND GETTING A JUMP

To play the outfield well, you must be prepared in mind and body. You must anticipate that every pitch will be hit and in what direction it will travel. Anticipating is how good outfielders get a "jump" on the ball. That is, it seems that they are moving, or jumping, in the direction of the ball a millisecond after it is hit. Doing so is probably even more important in the outfield than it is in the infield. To get a jump on the ball, you must be so focused on the pitch and swing that you find yourself moving toward where the ball is going to be hit even before the batter makes contact.

THE READY POSITION

It takes a little experience to develop this ability, but you will find it comes easily. Make certain you have your knees bent and that you're on the balls of your feet just as the pitch is being released. Keep your hands off your knees and be ready to move in any direction. When you find your body start to move with every pitch, trust your instincts. If you find yourself moving to either the left or the right, go with it.

THE ROUTINE FLY BALL

To catch a routine fly ball, one that is hit high enough for you to easily drift beneath it, judge where you think the ball is coming down, and move five feet behind that spot. Then take a few steps forward to make your catch. This forward momentum will be going in the direction of your throw, enabling you to have more power behind your throws. Catch the ball with two hands in front of your throwing shoulder. Using two hands will help you secure the ball in your glove, and catching it in front of your throwing shoulder will allow you to quickly move into the proper throwing position.

THE RUNNING CATCH

Running down a ball that flies over your head is difficult. You must learn to trust yourself enough to turn your back to the ball and sprint to the spot where you believe the ball will come down. To keep track of the ball's path, turn your head once as you're running and look at the ball. Once you near the ball, bring your body under control, relax, and catch the ball.

Fly Ball Basics

1. Anticipate where the ball will be hit.
2. Use two hands whenever possible.
3. Catch the ball with your glove-side foot slightly ahead.

When running back for a fly ball, drop your right foot back and turn your body. This allows you to run to the point of the ball's descent, rather than drifting or backpedaling.

Catch the ball with two hands over your throwing-side shoulder. Catching the ball on your throwing side puts you in better position to quickly grip the ball and make a throw to the infield.

4. Don't be afraid to turn away from the ball as you run to intercept it.
5. Know the direction and the strength of the wind.
6. Position yourself according to the game situation and the hitting tendencies of the batter.

MENTAL PREPARATION

Playing great defense requires more than physical skill. You must have a thorough understanding of game situations. Before each pitch you should keep the following in mind:

1. The inning
2. The score
3. The number of outs
4. The hitting tendencies of the batter
5. The foot speed of the batter and the base runners
6. What you will do with the ball if is hit to you (on the ground or in the air)

Hand the ball to your coach and sprint out toward center field. Every few steps, look over your shoulder (while running) to find the ball.

Extend your glove arm over your shoulder to catch the ball. Notice how the outfielder's eyes have followed the ball all the way into her glove.

Being mentally prepared for any scenario reduces defense to little more than catching and throwing. When you've reached that level of preparedness, you can call yourself a player.

DRILLS

Pass Receiver

This drill will develop the skill of catching the ball on the run. All of the players stand in a single-file line in the outfield. The coach stands parallel to the front of the line with a bucket of softballs at her feet. One at a time, each girl sprints straight out from the line, and the coach throws the ball to her, as if the coach is a quarterback and the player a wide receiver. Rotate the throws, high, low, left and right. After catching the ball, the player returns it to the bucket and runs back to her place in line.

In-Line Relay Race

This drill will develop throwing and catching skills, as well as transferring the ball from the glove to the throwing hand.

The squad is divided into two parallel lines about 30 feet apart, with an equal number of players in each. Each player in line stands 30 feet apart from the girl in front of and behind her. The player in the front of each line has a softball. On the coach's command or signal, the

The in-line relay race teaches proper footwork and a quick release. When receiving a relay throw, align your shoulders and feet (as shown) so they're in position to make an immediate throw.

front player turns and throws to the player behind her, who then throws it to the girl behind her. This continues until the player at the end of the line has received the ball. She then reverses the process, and begins throwing it back up the line. Players in the line who get the ball back to the lead (first) player win.

A Game of "31"

This drill is for increasing throwing accuracy. Break the team into groups of two, with each girl standing 30 feet away from and facing her partner.

- Player A throws the ball to player B, attempting to force Player B to catch the ball squarely in front of her face or her chest.
- If B catches the ball in front of her face, A receives 2 points.
- If B catches the ball in front of her chest, A receives 1 point.
- If B catches the ball in any other location, A receives 0 points.

Once Player B receives the ball, she throws the ball to Player A, attempting to hit the same targets. The first player to 31 points wins

A face shot earns the team two points.

the game. (You may increase or decrease the distance between the players according to their ability level.)

Around the Horn

This drill is to improve catching and throwing skills.

Divide the squad into four teams of four, with each squad having a player stationed at home plate, first base, second base, and third base. One team at a time, the ball is thrown around the diamond, from catcher to third to second to first to catcher. Each team continues until the ball touches the ground. For every base the ball safely reaches, the team of four receives one point. Once the ball touches the ground, switch teams. The team who gets the most bases before the ball touches the ground wins the game.

Double Plays

This drill is for infielders only and provides practice in fielding ground balls, making the double play, and perfecting various types of throws.

Station a player at each of the four infield positions. Hit ground balls to each player, beginning with the third baseman. The player must field the ball cleanly and throw it to the player covering second base, who then relays the ball to the first baseman to complete the double play.

Continue around the infield until each player has initiated the double play at least 10 times. Have the middle infielders—shortstops and second basemen—alternate the types of throws they use: overhand, underhand toss, and backhand flip, according to the position in which they field the ball, and their distance from their teammate covering second base.

THE POSITIONS

4

There is more to playing defense than just fielding ground balls, catching fly balls, and throwing accurately. You've got to know your position inside and out. Each position has unique responsibilities that require attention and execution. In this chapter, you'll learn that playing defense with your head is just as important as having a sure-handed glove and strong throwing arm.

It's also important that you absorb as much information as possible about every position. This enables you to play multiple positions, thus increasing your value in the eyes of your coach and teammates. In some cases, you may be called on to fill in for an injured or missing player at a position you're not accustomed to playing. Knowing the demands of each position ahead of time will simplify the transition of playing defense in "foreign territory."

First we'll discuss what many consider to be the most important position on the field. The catcher is often referred to as the field general and is a player who must have a directive presence on the field. We'll move on to each infield position and then review the outfielders. The responsibilities of the pitcher are discussed in detail in Chapter 5: Pitching.

THE CATCHER

Former Princeton University head softball coach Cindy Cohen once said, "I do not think you can have a good team without a good catcher." That's a profound statement coming from an individual who won 560 Division I college softball games, guided Princeton to 12 Ivy

Running catches and diving stops entail more than physical ability. You've got to know your position on the field to be a standout defensive player.

League titles and two Women's College World Series appearances in 1995 and 1996. Pitching and defense win softball games, but both of those aspects rely heavily on the ability of the girl stationed behind home plate. Catchers can make a good pitcher great, and a solid defense spectacular.

Although her face hides behind a mask, the catcher must be the most visible and vocal player on the field. The title "catcher" calls out the most rudimentary obligation of numerous tasks. True, a catcher must catch the ball first and foremost. But a catcher must also be a leader, a director, an orchestrator, and a strategist. She has to maintain control of the game, its tempo, and its personality. The best catchers are those who contribute to their team physically, mentally, and emotionally.

Equipment

It's obvious that the catcher has a unique role just by comparing her appearance to the other defensive players. She wears shin guards, a chest protector, a larger glove, a helmet, and a face mask. She looks as if she's preparing herself for warfare.

It's important to wear the proper equipment at all times when catching. This means wearing your shin guards, chest protector, helmet, and mask every time take your position—practice and game alike. It is equally important to wear equipment that fits. The equipment is worn to ensure safety and protect you from injury. If your equipment is too big (and loose), balls will nestle their way into unprotected areas. If your equipment is too small (and tight), parts of your body will be uncovered and at risk of being struck by a ball. Obtain and wear equipment that fits your body specifically. It will be more comfortable to play in, but most importantly, it will provide optimum protection and safety.

Always wear your equipment when catching. This includes practice and bullpen sessions. A ball is just as likely to take a bad bounce in practice as it is in the game. Besides, you should train in the gear you'll be wearing during competition. By not wearing your shin guards or mask for example, you'll be less aggressive and develop poor habits that will come back to haunt you during a game.

GLOVE

Catcher's gloves are obviously different in size and shape than infielder and outfielder gloves. They are made larger so that you can scoop and block balls in the dirt. The pockets are also deeper, which protects your glove-hand from stinging when catching a ball from a pitcher who throws hard.

Finding a suitable glove is essential. As mentioned, catcher's gloves are bigger, but don't purchase a glove that is too big or heavy for you to handle. Because pitchers are throwing balls that drop, rise, tail, or curve, quick hands are a primary function of reliable catchers. A low and outside fastball in the dirt is difficult to snare if your glove is oversized. Much like selecting a bat, find the largest glove you can handle without diminishing your hand speed behind the plate.

The Catcher's Stance

The catcher's stance can be an uncomfortable position, but to condition your legs to catch an entire game, use it all the time. Blocking balls, throwing out runners, and fielding bunts becomes much more difficult to execute if your legs grow tired late in the game. Use the catcher's stance in practice and during bullpen sessions.

To assume the position, place your feet slightly narrower than shoulder-width apart. Lower your body by bending at the knees. Your rear end should nearly touch the ground. Lean forward with your upper body so that your chest rests over your knees. The weight of your body rests on the balls and toes of your feet, with your heels raised in the air.

A good target is very helpful to the pitcher. Also, starting the glove in the proper position helps you to catch pitches thrown to varying locations. Hold the glove up near your midsection in the center of your body. Move it about one foot out in front of your body, so it's held slightly in front of your knees. Allow your elbows to hang over your knee caps or slightly outside of them. Do not let your elbows pinch inside of your knees. This restricts the mobility of your arms and can impede your path to the pitch. Hold your throwing hand behind your glove so it's protected.

Some catchers like to hold their throwing hand behind their back or down behind their ankle. This is okay, but when runners are on base, it takes more time to get the ball out of the glove. The throwing hand has to come around the body and to the glove, which adds time to the release.

This photo illustrates the catcher's stance. Keeping the throwing hand behind your back shields it from foul tips.

Position yourself behind the plate as close to the batter as possible without getting hit. This should be about an arms-length away. Squatting too far behind home plate gives the impression that strikes are actually low and out of the strike zone. Also, a greater number of pitches will land in the dirt, where they're more difficult to block.

Receiving the Pitch

Now that you're set up properly, it's time to catch the pitch. Catching the ball not only keeps base runners from advancing, but it also helps the pitcher. A good defensive catcher enables the pitcher to pitch with increased confidence. Not having to worry about balls getting past the catcher stimulates the pitcher's desire to be more aggressive with her pitches. In addition, receiving the ball correctly improves the presentation of the pitch. This may sway the opinion of the umpire and earn more called strikes.

When receiving the ball, consider the pitch being thrown. If it's a fastball, the ball will stay straight. Drop pitches will dip, while curveballs will break to the right or left depending on whether the pitcher is right- or left-handed. Know what pitch is coming so you're not taken by surprise.

From the stance position, make sure you have some flex in your glove-side elbow when holding up your target. Do not stiffen or straighten your arm when receiving the pitch. Balls are likely to pop out of your glove. To have soft hands, allow for a little "give" when receiving the ball. Never stab at the ball, or make any violent movements to catch it. Unless the pitch is thrown wildly, stay relaxed and follow the pitch all the way into the glove.

Try to catch everything with the glove pointed upward. If you turn the glove over and catch the ball with the fingers pointing down, chances of getting a called strike are slim. If the pitch is very low to your glove-side, turn the glove over to catch the ball. All other pitches should be caught with the fingers pointing up or to the side.

FRAMING PITCHES

Because calling balls and strikes is fairly subjective, the catcher can assist the pitcher in how she catches pitches. This is called "framing pitches." Framing means receiving a pitch that is on the border of or just outside the strike zone and turning your glove inward, upward, or downward toward the strike zone. For example, if a right-handed hitter is at the plate and the pitch is a little inside, roll your wrist inward (toward home plate) as you catch the pitch. Because everything happens so fast, framing the pitch may give the umpire the illusion that the pitch actually crossed over the inside part of home. Strike one!

Get in the habit of doing this all the time. Practice during bullpen sessions. Cradle every pitch you receive toward the strike zone. It can really help your pitchers get a few extra called strikes each game.

To frame a pitch, turn the glove inward towards the strike zone (or home plate) as you catch the ball.

SETTING UP ON THE OUTSIDES OF THE PLATE

As you advance to higher levels of play, get into the habit of setting your target up over both sides of the plate. This does not simply mean to move your glove to a particular corner, but instead, shifting your feet and your entire body. Setting up your catcher's stance on the outsides of home plate can help expand the strike zone. Strikes on the corner appear to catch the middle of the plate, and with the help of framing, pitches just off the plate may be called strikes.

Most youth league catchers get into their catcher's stance directly behind the middle of home plate and hold their glove over the middle of the plate. This is because most young pitchers are shaky with their control. The problem is that if a pitch crosses the plate on the inside or outside corner, the catcher has to move her glove to the right or left to receive the pitch. This gives the umpire the impression that the pitch is off target, causing him or her to call it a "ball."

To help a pitcher who has good control, set up in your stance so that the corner lines up with the middle of your body. With the glove perched over the corner of the plate, pitches slightly outside or inside look pretty good to the umpire. By then framing a pitch just off the plate, you begin to expand the strike zone.

So if you're calling for a pitch on the outside corner, move your feet over so that your body is aligned with the outside corner. It could prove to be the difference between a ball and a called strike.

BLOCKING BALLS

Blocking balls in the dirt is a vital skill that you must master. It keeps runners from advancing bases or potentially scoring. Becoming proficient at blocking balls also allows your pitcher to throw with confidence. This is something that won't show up in the stats book, but will be discernible in the pitcher's performance.

There are two methods of blocking pitches. One method is for blocking pitches in the dirt in front of you. The other is for blocking pitches that are wild, low, and to the side. For pitches that are in front of you, kick your legs back and drop to your knees. Your knees should now be in the same spot that your toes once were. Hunch your shoulders inward and lean forward. You want to surround the ball and trap it in case it bounces upward. From this position, the ball will drop straight down in front of you. Do not lean back because the ball can then carom off your midsection and get away from you. Runners advance.

On a pitch in the dirt, turn your glove over so the fingers point downward. (Imagine an infielder catching a ground ball.) Keep the glove in contact with the ground, so the ball can't scoot underneath and roll under your legs. Keep the glove down and your head down. Do your best to catch the ball, but remember your primary objective is to stop the ball from getting past you. Never attempt simply to catch pitches in the dirt when there are runners on base. Immediately drop to your knees to block the pitch when you see it is low. If you happen to catch it clean, that's a bonus.

If the ball is a little to the side (inside or outside), shift your entire body in that direction as you drop down to your knees. Your upper body can act as a shield and prevent balls from bouncing past you.

To block pitches that are wild to side, kick your leg out diagonally toward the first or third baseline (depending on the location of the pitch). Fold your opposite-side knee down and inward toward home plate, keeping your rear end and chin

When blocking a pitch in the dirt, drop to your knees and lean forward with your upper body. Shift your body (laterally) to keep the ball in the middle of your body.

down. This gives you the best chance of blocking a pitch that is difficult to handle.

Practice blocking balls every day, so dropping to your knees becomes instinctive. When doing so, have a coach or teammate throw the balls underhand to simulate the true bounce the ball will take. The ball will bounce differently if it's thrown overhand. And remember, wear all of your equipment.

FIELDING BUNTS

Because sacrifice bunting plays such a major role in fastpitch softball, it is imperative that catchers are competent in fielding bunts. When a hitter squares around to sacrifice bunt, she's *sacrificing* an out to advance the runner. It's critical that you take advantage of that sacrifice every time. A good fielding catcher also allows the first and third basemen to play a little deeper, which helps increase their range in the field.

Fielding Foul Pop-Ups

Another opportunity to collect an easy out is catching a foul pop-up. A foul pop-up occurs when a hitter contacts the very bottom of the ball, sending it straight up in the air in foul territory behind the catcher. The catcher has to find the ball, position herself under the landing point of the ball's descent, and secure it for an out.

Pop-ups behind home plate will always carry back toward the infield. Factor this into where you set up for the catch, and squeeze the ball with two hands.

The first step at catching this type of hit is finding the ball. Hopefully, your teammates will be of assistance and call out where the ball is located. Once the ball is hit, stand up out of the squat position, and turn your back to the infield. Take off your mask and hold it in your throwing hand. When you find the ball, run over to its general location and throw the mask far off to the side. (When throwing the mask, toss it is as if you were throwing a Frisbee.) If you drop the mask or just flip it to the side, you'll risk tripping over it when making the catch.

You've found the ball, tossed your mask to the side, and are now standing under the ball. All that is left is to squeeze it in your glove, right? Not exactly. Once you're positioned directly under the ball, take two steps back toward the infield. Because the ball is hit with back-spin, it will carry back toward the infield. Factor this in every time you set up in a spot to catch a foul pop.

When making the catch, always use two hands. The catcher's mitt was not designed for catching balls falling from the sky and they can pop out. Use two hands to secure the ball in the glove. After making the catch, turn toward the infield, and check for runners on base. They might try to tag up.

Defending the Steal

Sacrifice bunts advance base runners into scoring positions. Stealing a base allows runners to advance without sacrificing an out at the plate. It's the catcher's responsibility to stop the running game and keep runners in check.

In baseball, runners can leave the base at any time. If a pitcher has a slow delivery to the plate, the runner can steal on the pitcher. This means their delivery is so slow that the catcher has absolutely no chance of throwing the runner out. In softball, the runner cannot leave the base until the pitch is released. That means the responsibility of thwarting the opposition's running game lies squarely on the catcher's shoulders.

Many believe that a catcher must possess a strong arm to throw runners out. A strong arm certainly helps, but there are many other critical factors involved. Catchers must anticipate runners stealing and prepare by adjusting their stance. They must have quick footwork to swiftly get into throwing position. The time it takes them to transfer the ball from glove to hand and release the throw is crucial to cutting down runners. A strong arm is a great asset, but these other elements weigh heavily into whether the runner slides in safely or dejectedly trots back to the dugout.

With runners on base, adjust your stance by raising your rear end up. Don't sit down in your squat, but rather remain perched so you can quickly shift your feet if the runner steals. If you sit down, you have to rise up and then shift your feet, which adds time to your release.

RUNNER STEALING SECOND

When the runner is stealing second base, begin to move your feet as you catch the ball. Shift your feet so they are aligned to second base. This is accomplished by taking a short step forward with your rear foot so that it's parallel to the pitching rubber. Follow by taking a short step

Quick feet are equally important to a strong arm when defending an attempted steal. Before releasing the throw, align your feet to the target.

The strong arm of a catcher can eliminate the threat of an opposing team's running game.

forward with your front foot. This acts as your step to throw.

By shifting your feet, your hips and shoulders are now aligned with the target and your body is in the throwing position. Don't stand up, but rather remain crouched by maintaining flex in your legs.

As you're shifting your feet into position, transfer the ball from glove to hand. Take the ball from your glove as your hands move back toward your rear shoulder. Your throwing arm continues back as you cock your arm to throw. Do not drop your arm down to throw in this situation. It takes too much time. Your arm should cock straight back as if you were pulling a bowstring to shoot an arrow.

Lock your eyes on the target and fire the ball on a line to the base. If you can't reach the base on a line, bounce the ball to the bag. It takes less time than if you were to send a high, arcing throw to the base. Also, always throw to the base, never the position player. The player will have time to get into position (at the base), while the ball is traveling.

RUNNER STEALING THIRD

With a runner attempting to steal third base, the principles are basically the same. Get yourself into throwing position quickly and make a strong, accurate throw to the base. The footwork, however, is simpler.

Instead of making a 90 degree turn to the right to align yourself to second base, you make a 45 degree turn to the left to take aim at third base.

As you receive the ball, shift your feet to the left so you're aligned to third base. Transfer the ball from glove to hand and fire a strike to the third baseman. This throw is shorter, but must be accurate. An errant throw can result in a run scored.

Where a right-handed batter takes her stance can influence your footwork. If the batter is deep in the box, step in front of the batter to throw the ball. If she's up in the box, step behind the batter to throw. At times, the batter may stand directly in your path. Use your lead arm to push the batter to your left and out of the way. If the batter is still in your way, the umpire should call interference.

FIRST BASEMAN

The importance of the pitcher and catcher to a team's defense is immeasurable. But once the ball is put in play, no player is more involved in a play's outcome than the first baseman. During the gold medal game in the 2000 Olympics in Sydney, Australia, American first baseman Sheila Douty had 11 putouts in the 2-1 victory over Japan. Granted, winning pitcher Lisa Fernandez struck out eight while limiting the opposition to three hits, but Douty was counted on to squeeze 11 crucial outs.

To play first base, you have to be smart, agile, sure-handed, and instinctive. Make the wrong decision and the runners are safe all around. Be in the wrong position and opposing offenses will exploit your whereabouts. Fail to catch the ball and you'll grant the offense those game-altering extra outs.

The most significant aspect of playing first base is catching throws from the infielders. Ground balls make up a substantial amount of batted balls, so plays at first occur with great frequency. Proper footwork and a sure-handed glove is the foundation of an adequate first baseman.

Standard Position

Positioning is determined by the game situation. If you find yourself standing in the same spot for every batter, you're not being attentive. As the game moves, keep your brain moving along with it.

First basemen often play in close to take away the bunt or slap hit. In this case, move approximately 10 to 15 feet in front of first base. Position yourself a crossover step away from the foul line. This allows you to stop any balls hit directly down the first base line. To check, get into your infielder's stance and take a crossover step with your right foot. Reach out with your glove and see if you can reach the foul line. If your glove is right at the foul line, you're in the perfect position. If not, adjust accordingly.

Against stronger hitters who are not likely to bunt or slap hit, move back a few steps. This will broaden your range. Move farther off the line so that it takes you two crossover steps to reach the foul line. Standing back farther from home plate affords you more time to react and get to balls hit to your right and left.

DEFENDING THE BUNT

U.S. Olympic Team first baseman Sheila Douty sets up nearly halfway to home plate in bunt situations. The closer you move in, the better chance you have of fielding the ball and forcing out a lead runner. As the pitch is being delivered, creep up toward home plate, staying low to the ground. As soon as you see the batter drop her hands to bunt the ball, charge in toward home plate.

Field the ball using two hands and listen to the call from your catcher and infielders. If they yell, "first, first, first" or "one, one, one," throw the ball to first base. If they yell, "second, second, second" or "two, two, two," throw the ball to second. Because your back is to the infield when you're fielding the ball, let your teammates be your eyes for the play and listen to their guidance.

With a runner on first base, a bunt play is a distinct possibility. Move in toward home plate to defend the bunt.

An accurate relay throw can keep a run off the scoreboard and your team in the game.

CUTOFFS AND RELAYS

With a runner on second base, move into the cutoff position on balls hit to center and right field. On hits to center field, move to a spot between the pitcher's mound and second base. On hits to right field, the cutoff position is the area between first base, the pitcher's mound, and the second base position. The exact position depends on the depth and location of the hit. It is the catcher's job to put you in a direct line between the ball and home plate.

The first baseman moves into the cutoff position for three reasons. First, she acts as a intermediate target for the outfielder. Outfielders are told to aim for the cutoff's head. Secondly, the cutoff player can step in and catch the ball if it's off-line. This restricts other base runners from advancing. Lastly, if the throw from the outfield is too weak, the cutoff player can intercept it, turn to home plate, and fire a short-range throw.

When setting up in the cutoff position, face the outfielder and hold your arms up in the air. As the ball travels toward you in the air, shift your feet so they are aligned for a throw to home plate. At this point, you'll be standing sideways to the ball. Catch the ball with two hands, turn your upper body to home plate, and send a crisp, accurate throw to the catcher.

THE BASIC INFIELDER'S POSITION

Part of fielding a ground ball is getting into the proper position before the ball is hit. To do this, start by spreading your feet farther than shoulder-width apart (slightly further than your batting stance). Bend at your knees and lower your rear end, while keeping your weight on the balls of your feet. Lean slightly forward with your upper body and extend your glove arm out in front of you. The glove should hover just above the ground with the palm facing upward.

Think of your feet and glove as a triangle. A line drawn between your feet makes up the base of the triangle and your glove is positioned at the apex of the triangle. Always try to field the ball near the apex of the triangle.

To make sure you arrive at this position before each pitch, develop a routine. What follows is a simple, five-step process to follow before every pitch.

- **Pick your spot**—Your defensive positioning depends on the situation. Are you at normal depth, double-play depth, or expecting a bunt? Does the hitter generally pull the ball or hit to the opposite field? Review the game situation to help determine your defensive positioning.
- **Make a decision**—Always know where you're going to throw the ball before it's hit to you. What base you throw to may depend on where the ball is hit. For example, if you're a second baseman and there is a runner on first base with one out, you're throwing to second base for the double play. However, if the ball is hit far to your left, the play is at first base to make sure of an out.
- **Take a deep breath**—As the pitcher toes the rubber, take a deep breath. This relaxes your body and allows you to focus on the job at hand.
- **A forward step**—Taking a step forward puts you on the balls of your feet. It moves your momentum toward the ball instead of sitting back and letting the ball play you. Infielders who stand still are flatfooted and fall back on their heels. This is a poor position from which to field the ball. Take a small step forward with either foot (it's personal preference) and bring the opposite foot forward so it's parallel.
- **Complete the triangle**—The final step is getting into the proper position. Bend the knees, lower the rear end, and extend the glove hand forward. Remember, a line drawn between the feet forms the base of a triangle and the glove rests at its apex.

Receiving the Throw at First Base

Most mistakes at first base are caused by faulty footwork. By following these simple steps, you can avoid misplaying throws because of your feet.

When the ball is hit on the ground, turn toward the infield and run to first base. By turning toward the infield as you run, you'll know to whom the ball is hit. This knowledge allows you to correctly square your body to the target. Assuming you're a left-handed first baseman, place your left foot on the base. The sole of your foot should press against the side of the base, while your toes rest on the ground. Your right foot

With your body square to your teammate, stand relaxed at first base as she makes her throw. Use this time to gauge the location of the ball.

Once you've recognized the throw is on target, step to the ball with your glove-side foot and catch the ball with two hands.

remains on the ground alongside of the left foot. As the throw is made, quickly assess the location of the throw. If it's directly at you, step straight ahead to the ball with your right foot. If it's off-line to the left, step in front of and across your left leg and reach across your body with your glove to make the catch. If the throw is off-target to your right, step to the right and extend your glove outward to make the catch.

Do not step or stretch for the ball before it is thrown. If the ball is not thrown where you've anticipated it, you'll get mixed up and have difficulty making the catch.

ERRANT THROWS

At times, throws are so far off-line that you can't stay on the base *and* catch the ball. In this case, leave the base. Your job is to stop the ball from getting past you and allowing the runner to advance an additional base. Don't attempt to hold the bag and catch a ball that's out of your reach.

On a throw that is way off-line to your left, you can attempt a catch-and-tag. When you see the ball is far left of the base, leave the bag and shuffle over to make the catch. As you catch the ball, swing your arm back in an attempt to tag the runner as she runs by. This is a tough play that requires great concentration. But as long as you catch the ball first, take a chance at tagging the runner. Your infielder will thank you when the inning is over.

Balls in the dirt are especially difficult to handle. Short hops can often be picked out of dirt with ease, but balls that bounce (farther in front of you) are tough to predict. Keep in mind that your job is to stop the ball. When challenged with a ball in the dirt, follow these three rules: 1) *Keep the glove low to the ground.* It's much easier to bring the glove up for a ball than it is to move it back down. Even if you don't catch the ball clean, by holding the glove low you can use the heel of the glove and your arm to block the ball. If the ball scoots under your glove, it's rolling all the way to the fence. 2) *Watch the ball all the way into your glove.* Players have a tendency to pick the head up on balls in the dirt. Keep your head down and watch the ball the entire time. It's very tough to catch what you can't see. 3) *Shift your body in front of the ball.* Whenever possible, move your upper body in front of the ball. If the ball skips or ricochets off your glove, your body will block the ball.

THIRD BASE

The third base position is often referred to as "the hot corner." Batted balls get to you in a hurry, so it's a position that requires very fast reactions. Third basemen should have good instincts, a strong throwing arm, and nerves of steel. Third base is not a place for a timid player.

Third basemen defend against a variety of offensive attacks. They have to field sacrifice and drag bunts. They combat slap hitters who attempt to sneak the ball in the hole between shortstop and third base, and also snare hard-hit smashes from powerful hitters in the middle of the line-up.

Standard Position

Where you set up in your fielder's position is dictated by the game situation, but for the majority of the time, stand five to 10 feet in front of third base. Using the basic fielder's position as a reference, spread your feet apart a few inches wider than usual. This lowers your center of gravity. There is minimal time to move laterally on the hard-hit balls, so it's important to start lower to the ground.

Be aggressive on ground balls. Always try to catch it clean, but at the very least, block the ball and keep it in front of you. Because the ball arrives so quickly, you can block it, pick the ball up, and still have time to throw the runner out at first base.

Field any balls you can get that are hit to your left (toward the shortstop hole). It's a much easier play for you make. Your momentum

Field any ball to your left that you can reach. It's an easier play for you to make than the shortstop and a much shorter throw.

is taking you closer to first base, while the shortstop is moving away from first base. Field everything you can reach.

DEFENDING THE BUNT

Bunters use the foul lines as targets, so the majority of bunts are to first and third base. In a bunting situation, move inward an additional 15 to 20 feet. Creep in slowly and look at the hitter's hands. If she drops them to bunt, break towards home plate. Try to field the ball just inside your left foot. This quickly aligns your feet and shoulders to first base. Field the ball with two hands and make an accurate throw to make sure of an out. If the catcher or infielder yells for you to throw to second or third base, shift your feet to align yourself with the base of choice.

On balls that are bunted to the first baseman, quickly retreat to third base. When executing the most common bunt coverage, the second baseman covers first base and the shortstop covers second base. This leaves third base unattended. Race back to third to prevent the first-base runner from advancing all the way to third base.

CUTOFFS AND RELAYS

On balls hit to the left field with runners in scoring position, the third baseman becomes the cutoff player for throws to home plate. Position yourself between the third baseline and pitcher's mound. (Adjust your depth to how shallow or deep the left fielder throws the ball.) Listen to the catcher's direction. It's her job to align you with the left fielder and home plate.

As the throw approaches, the catcher may yell, "Cut," which means to catch the ball and hold it. If she yells, "Cut four," catch the ball and throw to home plate. If she doesn't yell at all, let the ball continue on its path home. She also may yell, "Cut two" or "Cut three," which means to throw to second or third base.

MIDDLE INFIELDERS

Dot Richardson, Jennifer McFalls, Crystl Bustos. These women are among the best in the business when it comes to playing the middle-infield positions. They dazzle crowds with diving stabs, powerful throws, and lightning-quick double play turns.

Middle infielders play the shortstop and second-base positions. Players at these positions need to be very quick and agile. They patrol much of the infield territory, turn double plays, cover second base on steals, take cutoff throws from the outfield, back up bases, and rotate on bunt plays. No matter where the ball is hit, middle infielders are constantly moving to help out on defense.

Standard Position—Shortstop

At shortstop, position yourself between the second-base bag and the third-base bag. Because the third baseman will cover some territory to your right, move a step or two closer to second base. Don't play too close to second base, however, or you'll leave a large hole between you and the third baseman. In addition, balls to your backhand side are more difficult to field and throw to first base. By standing too close to second base, you'll field more balls to your backhand side.

If you were to stand in a direct line between second and third base (even with the bag), take three to four steps backward. This is the normal depth for you to play the shortstop position. With a fast runner at the plate or if you have a below-average throwing arm, move in a couple of steps. As with the other infield positions, game situations dictate the exact spot you'll play for each pitch. Always be aware of the game situation.

Standard Position—Second Baseman

At second base, position yourself between the second base bag and the first base bag. Because the first baseman covers some territory to your left, move a step or two closer to second base. This increases the amount of balls hit to your left, which are easier balls to field and throw.

Similar to the shortstop position, line up even with the bag and take three or four steps backward. You could even play a step or two deeper to increase your range. The short throw to first base affords you more time to make the play. At times during the game, you'll shift to the right or to the left, depending on the hitter and situation.

DEFENDING THE BUNT—SHORTSTOP

At shortstop, you'll cover second or third base for every bunt. Never get caught standing still on a bunt play. Which base you cover depends on the play coverage called by your coach. With a runner on first, and the first and the third basemen charging, cover second base. With runners at first and second base, you may cover second or third base. At times, the third baseman will stay at the base and the pitcher will cover bunts to the third base side. In this case, cover second base. Another coverage calls for the third baseman to charge aggressively in an attempt to field the ball quickly and force out the lead runner at third base. In this case, sprint to third base.

Always leave your position early enough to get to the base in time. In other words, anticipate the play. Get to the base early enough to give the thrower a target. Catching the ball on the run as the base runner arrives is risky business.

DEFENDING THE BUNT—SECOND BASEMAN

At second base, your job is to cover first base on sacrifice bunt plays. The first baseman plays in to field bunts to the right side, leaving first base open. Get to the base quickly for the sure out.

When the catcher fields a bunt near home plate, give her a clear throwing lane to throw through. To do this, hold the base with your left foot and position your body on the inside of the base. The catcher will be able to clearly see you, and won't hit the runner with her throw. Do not stand in line with the path of the runner.

CUTOFFS AND RELAYS

Shortstops and second basemen become cutoff players on balls hit to the outfield gaps. Anytime the batter hits a safe ball to an outfield gap, middle infielders move immediately to the outfield into cutoff position.

When setting up for the cutoff, always allow the outfielder to have the longer throw. Outfielder arms are conditioned and trained to throw the ball longer distances than infielders. On balls hit to the right side of second base, the second baseman goes out for the cutoff. The shortstop moves out for balls hit to the left side of second base.

If the batter hits a sure-double, meaning she'll definitely get to second base safely and may try for a triple, the opposite middle fielder becomes a back-up cutoff. For example, imagine a ball is hit left-center field and rolls all the way to the fence. The shortstop runs out and sets up in a cut-off position. Knowing the batter may try for a triple, the second baseman runs out and stands approximately 10 to 15 feet behind the shortstop. If the ball is overthrown or gets past the shortstop, the second baseman is in position to catch the ball.

Double Plays

Nothing shifts the momentum of a game more rapidly than a double play. The offense begins to sense a potential rally when runners reach base with only one out. The defense is aware that one big hit can give their opposition control of the game. But a ground ball double play to the infield quickly eliminates the chance of a big inning, and any hopes the offense has of putting a crooked number on the scoreboard instantly vanish.

DOUBLE PLAY FEEDS—SHORTSTOP

Quick feet and quick hands can turn one out into two. With a runner on first base and only one out, the double play is in order. The key to "turning two" is getting your body into position before the ball arrives. From there, it's simply execution.

In double-play situations, move a few steps in and over toward second base. When the ball is hit to you, square up to the ball (get in front

When throwing to second base from shortstop, field the ball, pivot, and make a quick, crisp throw. Do not stand up or shuffle your feet. It takes too much time.

of it) immediately. As you set your feet, open your left foot slightly toward second base. Field the ball with two hands, and from the crouched position, fire a crisp throw to the chest of the second baseman. Use a very short, quick release. Standing up to throw or a using a big armswing adds precious time. Never rush the throw, but be quick and efficient.

On balls that take you to your left, toss the ball underhand to the second baseman. Step toward her with your left foot and be deliberate. Allow her to see the ball. Toss the ball on a straight line. A toss with arc adds time.

DOUBLE PLAY FEEDS—SECOND BASEMAN

Move a few steps in and closer to second base. How you deliver the ball depends on where it is hit. On a ball hit directly at you, field the ball as you would regularly. As you glove the ball, dip your right knee inward and turn your hips and shoulders square to the target at second base. Stay low to the ground. Bring the ball straight up to the throwing position and fire a crisp throw to the chest of the shortstop.

On balls hit to your right, field the ball and toss it underhand to the shortstop. Step with your left foot and be deliberate. Allow the shortstop to see the ball. Toss the ball on a line with little or no arc.

On balls hit directly at you, pivot toward second base, dip your right knee, and throw the ball to the shortstop's chest.

Balls fielded close to second base can be tossed underhand to the shortstop. This is a quicker, safer method of starting the double-play turn.

When the ball is hit to your left, use good judgment. Getting the force-out at second base in this situation is a tough play to make. To execute this play, take a short hop to shift and rotate your feet into the throwing position. Field the ball off with your chest facing home plate. Shift your feet to the right by jumping up and turning your body to the right. Your back is now facing home plate and your chest is facing center field. Using a short release, fire a throw to the outside of second base.

DOUBLE PLAY TURNS—SHORTSTOP

When turning a double play from the shortstop position, always make sure of the first out. Too often, players try to catch and throw too quickly and drop the ball. Catch the ball first and then go for the out at first base.

Proper footwork and a quick release determine the outcome of your execution. On balls hit to the right side of the infield in double-play situations, get to the base quickly so you can set your feet. Arriving late forces you to do everything on the move, which makes things more difficult. To get to the base quicker, shade a few steps forward and to the left when taking your position.

There are two simple methods of turning double plays from shortstop position. The first is commonly used on routine balls hit to the second baseman. Stand right behind the base and hold your glove out in front of your chest for a target. As the throw travels on its path, shift your body forward and to the left, swiping the back of the base with your right foot. Catch the ball with two hands, step to the left and throw to first. This takes you out of the path of the runner. After throwing the ball, take a small hop in case the runner attempts to slide into your legs.

The second method is used on hard-hit balls or balls hit to the right of the second baseman. Because you'll have less time to get to the base, you accept the throw a step or two behind second base. As you catch the ball, step on the back of the base to stop your momentum forward and to protect you from the runner. This method is also used on balls hit to the first baseman. When this occurs, make sure you give the first baseman a clear lane to throw through. Do not set up in the path of the runner.

On double play turns from the shortstop position, stand behind second base and shift to the left as you receive the ball. This removes you from the path of the runner as you make the throw to first base.

Here are a few checkpoints to follow when turning a double play.

- *Get to the base as quickly as possible.* The sooner you get to the base, the more time you'll have to set your feet and get your body under control.
- *Wait to see the throw.* Anticipating a perfect throw is a mistake. If your body is moving in one direction and the throw is off-line, you won't be in good position to field the throw. See the ball first, and then move your feet.
- *Catch the ball with two hands.* This makes transferring the ball from glove to hand quicker and more efficient.
- *Square your shoulders to the target.* Throwing on the move is an advanced skill. Squaring your shoulders allows you to throw accurately with greater consistency.
- *Hop after the throw.* The job of the base runner is to slide into your feet to alter your throw. Once the ball is released, a short hop can help you avoid being tripped up and risking injury.

DOUBLE PLAY TURNS—SECOND BASEMAN

Turning double plays from second base is tough because you're moving away from first base to receive the throw and then have to turn and face the opposite direction to throw. Getting to the base quickly is the most important step in turning double plays from second base. It affords you the time to stop your momentum, set your feet, and align your shoulders with first base.

When turning a double play from the second base position, receive the ball with your left foot on second base (left). As you make the catch, step back off the base with your left foot, plant on your right foot, and throw to first base.

In double-play situations, move a few steps inward and over toward second base. Where the ball is hit will determine your footwork.

- *Balls hit to the right of the shortstop or third baseman.* On balls hit to the right of the shortstop or fielded by the third baseman, come across the base as you receive the throw. Facing your team-mate, step on the base with your left foot. As the ball is traveling to you, step across the base and catch the ball as your right foot touches the ground. Plant on that leg, pivot and throw to first base. Planting on your right foot as you catch the ball allows a quick release.
- *Balls hit at the shortstop or to her left.* Stay behind the base so that your back faces right-center field. Step on the base with your left foot as you await the throw. As the ball is delivered, step back with your left foot, catch the ball, and throw to first base. Focus on a strong follow-through to ensure an accurate throw.

OUTFIELD

Outfielders see less action than infielders, but the impact of the plays they're involved in can change the face of a game. A spectacular play in the outfield can thwart an offensive rally, but a mishap can open the gates to an onslaught of runs.

Most outfielders are able to catch simple fly balls, but the elite ones get great jumps. This enables them to cover more outfield territory. The only way to develop this sense of anticipation and instinct is by taking thousands and thousands of fly balls off of the bat.

The best time to practice playing outfield is during batting practice. There, you'll get a true feel for how the ball comes off the bat off of a live pitch. Use batting practice wisely and work on getting good jumps.

Standard Position

The left, right, and center fielders stand in different locations in the outfield, but they should all be set in similar positions. As the pitcher winds up, focus on the batter. When the pitch is released, take a step forward and assume the athletic position—feet shoulder-width apart, knees flexed, weight on the balls of your feet, slightly bent at the waist. Hold your glove out in front of you with the palm facing the sky and be ready to move in any direction.

Each hitter will dictate where you stand in the outfield. When defending a power hitter, the entire outfield plays a few steps deeper. If it's a slap hitter at the plate, move a few steps in toward the infield.

There are also pull hitters and opposite field hitters that may force you to adjust your location. For example, if a left-handed hitter pulls the ball consistently, each outfielder shifts over toward the right-field line. Pay attention to what your fellow outfielders are doing to ensure you're defending each hitter alike.

The left fielder has an important job if a slap hitter is at the plate. If you're a left fielder, play very shallow and toward the left-field line. Slap hitters sometimes mishit the ball and lift it into the air. Because they take abbreviated swings, the ball drops in just over the heads of the third baseman and shortstop. An attentive left fielder can take this hit away by playing shallow and anticipating the play.

ALWAYS CHECK THE WIND

Wind has a profound effect on the flight of fly balls. Always know the direction of the wind and how it will affect balls hit in the air. The wind can blow in, out, or across the field. Pick up some grass before each hitter bats and flip it up in the air. This direction the grass blows indicates the wind's direction.

CUTOFFS AND RELAYS

Throwing accurately to cutoff players is an extremely important aspect of playing the outfield. By throwing the ball directly on-line to your cutoff players, you'll stop base runners from advancing extra bases and may even throw a few out.

On extra base hits, run to the ball as fast as you can. You should have an idea of where the cutoff player will set up by knowing the game situation, runners on base, and length of the hit. After picking up the ball, quickly find your teammate, step directly at her, and fire the ball to her glove. A quick release is important. For every additional step you take to throw the ball, the base runner is gaining two strides.

When the play is to home plate, get to the ball as quickly as possible. If the hit is in front of you, sprint to the ball and then break down in the final few steps to get your body under control. Use the "do or die" (covered in Chapter 3) method to make this play. Again, fielding the ball and releasing it in the shortest possible amount of time increases your chances of throwing the runner out.

Lock your eyes on the cutoff player and throw the ball to her on a line. If you miss her or overthrow her, the run will score and the batter will advance another base. A strong throw serves your team well, but only if it's on target.

Whenever you're throwing directly to a base, aim low. A low throw allows the receiving infielder to apply her tag swiftly. Also, if your throw is a little off (vertically), it's better to miss low than to miss high. The receiver has a chance of picking the ball out of the dirt and then applying a tag. If the ball is over her head, she has no chance of making a play.

BACKING UP BASES

Infielders get more action, but as an outfielder, always move with the play. Backing up bases minimizes the damage inflicted by errant throws. To back up a base, align yourself behind the target with the thrower. Stay at least 30 to 40 feet behind the receiver so you have time to react to the erratic throw.

Throw the ball on a direct line to the cut-off player. Think about throwing the ball through the cut-off player's chest.

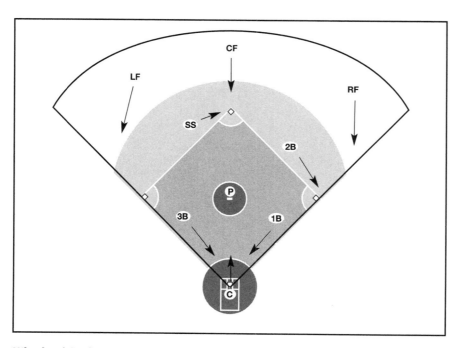

Whether it's a bunt or a play or regular ground ball to the infield, outfielders should be moving on every play to back up players and bases.

Any time there is a play in the infield, at least one of the outfielders should be moving to back up a throw. Throws from the first baseman and second baseman, to second base and third base should be backed up by the left fielder. The left fielder also backs up throws to third base from the catcher and pitcher during bunt and steal attempts. Throws to second base from the shortstop and third baseman are backed up by the right fielder as are balls thrown to first base by the pitcher and catcher. Balls thrown by the catcher and pitcher to second base are backed up by the center fielder.

Lastly, outfielders need to back up each other. The center fielder backs up both the right and left fielder on ground balls and fly balls. The wing outfield positions back up the center fielder on plays closer to their respective sides as well.

DON'T DIVE TO THE LINES

If you play left or right field, diving for a ball that is on your foul-line side is ill-advised. That means balls falling to your right if you're a left fielder or to your left if you're a right fielder. The problem is that the center fielder can't back you up. If the ball gets by you, it will probably roll all the way to the fence. By the time you get up, run back to the fence, and throw the ball to the infield, the batter may have already circled the bases. Only dive for a ball toward the line if the game is at stake.

Diving for balls hit to the gaps is a smarter, aggressive play. Your center fielder can easily back you up, so it's a sensible risk. Diving toward the lines is gamble that could prove fatal to your team.

GAMES

Softball in the Barrel

Position all the outfielders in a single-file line in right field. Place a plastic barrel on its side in front of third base and home plate, with the openings facing right field. Hit fly balls and ground balls to each outfielder and have her attempt to throw the ball into the barrels, first throwing to third, then to home. Points are awarded according to the accuracy of the throws: any throw within three feet of the barrel earns one point; any throw that strikes the barrel without going in earns two points; any throw that goes into a barrel earns three points. Move outfielders to different positions in the outfield to keep the game interesting.

With each player positioned at the point of a star, roll grounders back and forth. Focus on reaching for the ball and keeping your rear end down.

The main benefit from this game is improved throwing accuracy and trajectory. It encourages outfielders to keep their throws down instead of unleashing high-arcing throws that are inefficient. Also, consistent throwing from the outfield will improve the player's arm strength.

Five Star Grounders

Position five players such that each represents one point on a star. With one softball amongst the group, each player readies herself in the basic fielder's position. The game starts when a player rolls a grounder to the player two positions to her left. That player then rolls a grounder to the player two positions to her left, and so on. After each player has fielded six or eight balls, change the direction of the game by rolling grounders to the player two positions to the right. Each player should track their progress by counting the number of balls they field cleanly each time they play the game.

Five Star Short Hops

This game is similar to Five Star Grounders, only players deliver short-hops to one another instead of ground balls. Players should deliver an overhand toss that bounces a foot in front of the fielder. This game

Field short-hops thrown from close range by your teammates. Concentrate on keeping your glove low to the ground and "giving" with the ball to develop soft hands.

teaches players to develop soft hands and keep the ball in front of them at all times.

DRILLS

The Goalie Game

Have the catcher put on all of her protective equipment and assume her position at home plate. Behind her, place a goalie net, preferably a street hockey goal. Any type of configuration that is four feet high by four feet wide is ideal.

With the goal placed just behind the catcher, pitch balls in the dirt from close range (approximately 30 feet). The catcher's objective is to block the ball and not allow any pitches to go in the net. Work on the catcher's technique for getting her body in front of balls in the dirt, sliding side to side, and making sure that she uses her glove to block the hole between her legs. Count the number of goals the catcher allows in 20 pitches to monitor her progress.

Pop Fly Priorities

Send all of the fielders out to their positions except for the pitcher and catcher. With a tennis racquet and tennis ball, serve pop flies into the shallow outfield, covering the area from foul line to foul line. Hitting tennis balls with a racquet makes it much easier to place balls in the most troublesome areas.

Infielders and outfielders chase for balls and must call out to make the catch. This drill aims to develop communication skills amongst infielders and outfielders. If a player wants to make the catch, she must call out, "Mine! Mine! Mine! Mine!" All other fielders should immediately peel off away from the play. If two players call for the ball, the outfielder always has priority. Because it's easier to catch the ball running in rather than running out, the outfielder outranks the infielder on pop flies.

Knockout

This drill is for infielders and helps to improve two skills: fielding ground balls and throwing accuracy.

Station one player at first base and the rest in a single-file line at the shortstop position. One player steps out of the line wearing a catcher's glove. (A catcher's glove is much more difficult to field ground balls with and forces the player to use two hands.) The coach hits a ground ball to her, and the player must field the ball cleanly and throw it to first base. If she doesn't field the ball cleanly or make a good throw—if it goes over the first baseman's head, for example—the player is knocked out of the game. Otherwise, she moves to the back of the line to wait for her next turn. Continue the game until only one girl remains. She is the winner.

Using a catcher's glove makes the game of Knockout more challenging.

The name of the game in fast-pitch softball is pitching.

5

PITCHING

The 2001 NCAA Division I Women's Collegiate World Series championship game pitted two of the nation's best pitchers against one another. Jennie Finch of the University of Arizona toed the rubber for the Wildcats, while Amanda Freed took the mound for the UCLA Bruins. Finch boasted a 31-0 pitching record entering the game, and Freed had yet to surrender a run during the World Series tournament.

With the score predictably deadlocked at 0-0 in the fourth inning, Arizona's Lindsay Collins drove a pitch from Freed over the right-center field fence to give the Wildcats a 1-0 lead. The lone run was all Finch needed as she shut down the Bruins offense en route to her 32nd consecutive win, and more importantly, the national championship. It marked Arizona's sixth national title and capped off a 65-4 season that included 42 shutouts.

The battle between Finch and Freed was one that will be talked about for many years. Their outstanding performances, however, represent much more than two talented pitchers going head-to-head in a championship game. The 1-0 score exemplifies the fiber of women's fast-pitch softball. Pitching dominates the sport. Superb pitching supported by solid defense will flourish at every level of the game.

Following the post-game celebration on the field, Finch stated, "It was just a matter of hitting my spots and using my defense." And that, in a nutshell, is the key to winning fast-pitch softball games. It may sound oversimplified, but it all starts with the pitcher throwing strikes.

THE INGREDIENTS OF A GOOD PITCHER

A superficial look at a pitcher discerns fastballs, change-ups, curveballs, riseballs, and drop pitches. A closer investigation, however, uncovers that pitching entails much more than physical ability. A girl who relies on her raw physical talent is simply a thrower. A girl who harnesses that talent and supplements it with mental competence and emotional discipline is a pitcher. To accomplish this, understand that good pitchers are guided by the three P's: Preparation, Poise, and Performance.

Preparation

Do you think Michele Smith, Christa Williams, or Lisa Fernandez just show up to the field and hope they have their 'A' game with them against international competition? No, I don't think so. They make sure they have their 'A' game by preparing for battle. Preparation plays a significant role in the success of a pitcher.

Ironing out mechanical flaws, establishing control of your pitches, and mastering your repertoire are all elements to be cared for during practice. Don't expect to refine your skills during pre-game warm-ups. Engine tune-ups are performed during practice and drill sessions.

It's important to be mentally prepared far ahead of the playing of our national anthem. Establish a game strategy so the competition only calls for execution. Are you going to get ahead with first-pitch fastball strikes? Or does this team first-pitch swing, convincing you to counter by throwing off-speed pitches low in the strike zone? Do their best hitters swing at pitches up and out of the strike zone, or are they apt to take called strikes on the outside corners? These are questions that should be answered before taking the field. The best way to defeat your opponents is to get to know them.

Positive visualization is a psychological exercise used to build confidence and a healthy frame of mind. Imagine yourself throwing pitches to perfect spots in the strike zone. Think back to the complete game shutout that you threw two weeks ago and feed off of that positive energy. Visualization helps you relax and pitch with confidence. Use it before a game, between innings, or during the game to enhance your performance.

Poise

Amongst the defensive fleet, the pitcher is the captain of the ship. She controls the tempo of the game, represents the backbone of the team's personality, and influences the outcome of the game more than any other player. To lead and lead successfully, the pitcher must display

Whether it's in the field, at the plate, or during practice, softball is a team game. It takes the contributions of nine players on the field to earn a victory.

poise through both good times and bad. Emotions can percolate during competition, but never allow them to rise too high or fall too low on the playing field.

Out on the battlefield, players exert maximum effort in hopes of gaining an advantage. Any time an individual gives it her all, expect human error to infiltrate the grounds. Elements beyond your control may not always go your way. Infielders and outfielders will make mistakes, opposing batters will hit balls in the hole and outfield gaps, your offense will struggle to score runs, umpires may call an inconsistent strike zone, and mental breakdowns will flare up in the heat of competition. You cannot govern these certainties of the game and must resist the adverse effects they can spawn.

Keep your cool on the mound. Consider the game is in your hands and your team cannot afford to have a crazed general leading the troops. Exhibiting poise entails keeping a serene expression on your face, mouthing only words of encouragement to teammates, maintaining positive body language, and staying focused on the job at hand rather than allowing less important factors to disrupt your concentration. It takes experience to develop poise, but the learning process can be accelerated by your willingness to mature.

ELIMINATING ACTIONS DISPLAYING A LACK OF POISE

1. Do not shout at or criticize your teammates.
2. Never argue with the umpire.
3. Do not shrug your shoulders, throw your arms in the air, or kick the dirt.
4. Don't react to the opposing team or spectators.
5. If batters are hitting you, don't simply try to throw harder.
6. Never jump for joy in success, nor sink to your knees in failure.
7. DO NOT trash-talk your opponents.

Performance

Performance is a result that relies heavily on being prepared and maintaining poise. Without those first two P's, performance suffers.

Any pitcher can throw strikes in the bullpen, participate in drills religiously, get batters out in scrimmage games, and remain positive before the game starts. Good pitchers, however, channel all of those elements into their performance and execution. Great performances are not always accomplished by following a blueprint, but rather by confronting the opponent and determining a method to defeat them. It's about making adjustments to their strengths and attacking their weaknesses. Your repertoire of pitches can get hitters out, but your heart and mind can beat them as well.

Confidence plays a major role in your performance. You've got to believe in yourself, expect to perform well, show faith in your ability, and will yourself to succeed. Confidence can carry you through a contest and it can also pull you out of a hole during a crucial situation. It can act as your crutch when things are going awry.

Always view performance as an opportunity. It's a chance to showcase your skills on the field, to display the hard work you've endured in training, to compete against a formidable foe, and to help your team win. Practice would be meaningless without the prize of competition, so embrace it with eagerness.

THE PITCHING FUNDAMENTALS

Much like hitting, pitching entails athleticism, tempo, and fluidity. Terms such as "fundamentals" or "mechanics" should be taken with caution. Your delivery is executed in one continuous motion to establish rhythm and power. Focusing on each mechanical movement as you pitch will produce disastrous results. Pitching in the game is a time for execution, not evaluation.

There may, however, be a breakdown during a certain portion of your delivery that needs to be isolated and repaired. That's why it's important to have an understanding of the proper mechanics. In times when you're experiencing problems with accuracy, velocity, or overall consistency, detecting and correcting a flaw in your delivery can steer you back on the path to success. The corrective action is accomplished through drills and repetitious training during practice. A game is not the time to harbor mechanical thoughts.

Read each part of the pitching delivery. By learning the basics, you'll eliminate some stumbling blocks en route to developing a proficient pitching motion. Some sections may simply work as checkpoints, while others will shed light on an element of your pitching motion that needs polishing. We've broken the pitching motion down into several fragments, but remember, the proper pitching motion is one continuous sequence of movements.

THE WINDMILL DELIVERY

The windmill delivery is the most common method of pitching in fast-pitch softball today. It is an underhand motion in which the pitching arm begins in front of the pitcher's body, moves in a long, backward circle, then descends forward until the ball is released at the hip. After the release, the arm continues upward to complete the follow-through.

The arm cannot work alone to manufacture the speed necessary to get hitters out. Try standing flat-footed and throwing a windmill pitch. You'll quickly notice your pitches lack sufficient velocity. You must wind up to generate some momentum that starts backward and then moves forward into your delivery. A long stride generates a wide base, which allows you to capitalize on the strength of your legs and torso. And as with hitting, weight shift and hip rotation permit you to drive your body forward through the delivery and generate maximum arm speed.

Mastering this delivery entails repetitious training. It's the only way to establish rhythm and tempo. The windmill delivery is reliant on a series of movements that lead up to a powerful release. If one of those movements falls out of sync, velocity and accuracy are sacrificed.

To throw a straight fastball, grip the ball across the seams. Hold the ball loosely in your fingers.

Grip

Your pitching grip depends on the type of pitch you're throwing, but in discussing the pitching motion, we'll deal strictly with the fastball. Grip the softball by placing your middle three fingers on top of the ball. Tuck your pinkie underneath the ball and rest your thumb on its side. The ball is held in the fingers, not in the palm. Jamming the ball back in your hand reduces velocity. Hold the ball securely in the fingers, but not too tight.

Grip the ball across the seams. This is called a four-seam fastball. It yields a straight pitch thrown at the highest possible velocity. For a four-seam grip, hold the ball so that the laces facing you form the letter C. Place your fingers across the C. (If desired, turn the ball so the laces form a backward C, whichever is more comfortable.) Because the rotation of the pitch travels in such a manner where the seams encounter wind resistance with greater frequency, the ball stays straight during its path to the plate.

The two-seamed grip reduces the velocity on your fastball slightly, but adds movement to your pitches. Turn the softball so that the seams form a horseshoe or "U" shape. Place your pointer finger and fourth finger along the seam and let your middle finger rest in between the seams. Because the rotation of the pitch travels in such a manner where the smooth sides of the ball encounter wind resistance with greater frequency, the ball moves on its path to the plate.

Learn to pitch with the four-seam grip first before experimenting with the two-seam grip. Develop maximum velocity and control before adding movement to your repertoire.

Pitcher's Stance

Much like a hitter initiates her swing from a batter's stance, a pitcher begins her delivery from a pitcher's stance. There is not one precise stance prescribed for all pitchers, but a basic stance puts you in position to more easily maintain proper mechanics throughout your motion.

Hold the ball in your glove and stand erect on the pitching mound. Your throwing-side foot rests on the pitching rubber with your toes extending over the edge of the rubber. (If you're right-handed, this is

Your pitcher's stance offers a time to relax and gain your composure. Review the purpose of your next pitch and visualize its successful result.

your right foot.) The toe of your opposite foot touches the back of the rubber. Bend your rear leg slightly, while keeping the front leg rigid. Stand with your feet positioned slightly narrower than shoulder-width apart.

With your arms resting near your midsection, square your shoulders to home plate and look in toward home plate with both eyes. Carry your weight on the balls of your feet and stand relaxed on the rubber. Shift your weight forward slightly as you take the sign from your catcher.

STEPS TO A SIMPLE PITCHER'S STANCE

1. Standing on the mound, review the situation. Note the score, inning, number of outs, runners on base, and the batter you're facing. Approach each pitch with a purpose in mind.
2. Hold the ball at your side. Step on the pitching rubber with your lead foot, extending your toes over the rubber. Toe the back of the rubber with your rear foot.
3. Allow your rear leg to bend slightly. The front leg remains rigid.
4. Square your shoulders to home plate, look in toward the catcher to take the sign. The catcher's signal should indicate the type of pitch and its location.
5. Visualize the pitch you're about to throw.
6. Take a deep breath and begin your wind-up.

Some pitchers opt to hold the ball down by their side outside of the glove. As they start their motion, they raise their hand and put the ball in the glove. This is okay as long you realize you have to adjust your

To initiate the motion, place the ball in your glove and rock back, shifting your weight onto your rear leg. Moving back builds up your momentum moving forward.

grip to the type of pitch you're throwing once the ball is placed in the glove. If you take your grip outside the glove, an observant hitter will notice your grip and decipher what pitch is coming before it's thrown, giving her a significant advantage.

Ignition—The Wind-Up

Before each pitch is delivered, build up some momentum that leads up to your release. This is accomplished during the wind-up. Your wind-up not only adds power to your pitches, but also creates commotion that can disrupt the hitter's vision and timing. The key to hitting is timing. The key to pitching is disrupting a hitter's timing.

To start, shift your weight back onto your rear foot. This is sometimes referred to as "rocking back." Lean back slightly with your upper body in a relaxed, controlled manner. Next, shift your weight forward onto the ball of your front foot. Keep your upper body tall and balanced over the pitching rubber. Your front leg should be flexed to accept the weight of your forward momentum. As you shift your weight forward, pull your arms inward toward your

Shift your weight back to your front leg to transfer your momentum forward. Keep your upper body balanced and over the pitching rubber.

midsection. Push them down (brushing your upper thigh) in a continuous, counter-clockwise motion as the lower half of your body moves forward, leading up to the stride. As you're about to take the stride, your upper body is tall, but leaned slightly forward over the rubber.

The Stride

The stride is an instrumental component to your pitching motion. It dictates the location of the pitch and also factors into how hard its thrown. It places the body in position from which it executes the final stages of your delivery.

The greater the stride, the more power you'll be able to generate.

As your weight shifts forward in your wind-up, your hands move inward and down in a counter-clockwise motion. With your weight balanced on your pivot foot, pick your stride foot up off the ground, bend, and extend your knee forward. Remove the ball from your glove and continue to begin your armswing backward.

At this stage, your front foot (still in contact with the pitching rubber) and stride foot are pointed at home plate. Your stride leg then extends forward toward home plate. Stride as far forward as possible, but keep your upper body tall. The longer the stride, the more power you're able to generate. While taking your stride, your glove arm extends forward.

OPENING THE HIPS

Once your stride leg is extended forward, open your hips. This means that you turn your hips inward toward your pitching arm side. To rotate sideways, pivot on the ball of your front foot. If you're a right-handed pitcher, your hip should open to face the third-base coach's box. If you're left-handed, open your hip to face the first-base coach's box.

Opening your hips is very important to generating power. As you release the pitch, you're going to fire your hips back to the closed position (facing home plate). This explosive hip torque engages the lower half of the body, and enhances your strength and arm speed. Think about underhand tossing a large bucket of water onto a fire. You'd first swing the bucket back, opening your hips and shoulders to generate some momentum. You'd then rotate your hips back closed to toss the

At this point in the delivery, the hips are open to home plate and face third base. Opening the hips harnesses the strength of your lower body, as they prepare to fire closed with the delivery of the pitch.

MAKE SURE YOUR FOOT IS ON TIME

Here's a reference to check and make sure your stride foot lands in the proper positioning. When your foot plants, imagine drawing a circle around it. The circle represents a clock and your foot is the hour hand. If you're a right-handed pitcher, your left foot should point to the 1:00 position. Any hour earlier than 1:00 and your hips will close prematurely, thus diminishing the degree of hip torque supplied in your delivery. Any hour later than 1:00 and your hips will be unable to fully rotate. A closed front foot blocks your hips from clearing and diminishes power.

For a left-handed pitcher, the stride foot should point to the 11:00 position. Any time earlier than 11:00 closes the hips off and restricts full rotation. If the stride foot points to a time later than 11:00, the hips open too early and lack explosiveness.

Take a look and check to see where your foot is pointing. You might pick out your problem just in the nick of time.

bucket of water. If your hips remained dormant and you simply relied on your arms, the water might not reach the flames. The reason for opening and closing your hips when pitching a softball is based on the same principle.

Stiff Front Leg

With your pitching arm reaching the peak of its backswing, the stride foot lands with the hips open. If you're a right-handed pitcher, your body is facing third base. Your leg is slightly bent when it lands, but it must quickly stiffen as you continue your motion. At the same time the pitching arm begins to swing down and forward, your weight transfers forward onto your front leg. The leg must be rigid in order to accept the weight of your momentum. If it remains bent, your weight will escape out in front of you, leaving you unable to generate explosive hip torque.

As your pitching arm swings forward and releases the ball, your hips immediately rotate and close. This clears a path for your arm to swing through and deliver the pitch, and also (as mentioned earlier) increases your arm speed. Your body's big muscles, namely the lower back, buttocks, thighs and abdominals, all contribute to your delivery when the hips fully rotate.

When the stride foot lands, the leg is initially bent. The bent leg allows your momentum to continue forward, just before the pitch is released.

As the pitch is released, the front leg stiffens. It accepts the weight transfer and acts as a post, allowing the hips to forcefully rotate. This generates maximum arm speed as the ball is released.

The Arm Circle and Release

As the stride foot lands, your body should form the shape of an "X" as viewed from the third-base position.

The wrist snap adds velocity to your pitch and increases the speed of the ball's rotation during its path to the plate.

Each fundamental step in the wind-up leads up to the release. Your lower body completes a series of movements to build momentum and get your body in a position to throw the ball with speed and accuracy. The arm acts like a whip in the windmill delivery, so keep it relaxed throughout the entire motion. Tension, or muscling up, slows the arm down.

When executing the arm circle, your pitching arm should travel along the same line throughout the arm swing. As the arm begins to move up (out in front of you), your palm faces downward. Imagine pulling a tissue out of a tissue box. This simulates the motion of the arm moving up and back.

As your arm continues back, rotate your shoulder open. This movement also begins to open your hips. As the shoulder rotates, your palm faces outward away from you. If you were to stop and look back at your hand, you should be able to look at your ring finger. Your arm is near extension, allowing a little flex in your elbow to stay relaxed.

If you were to stop your pitching arm when your stride foot landed, it should point out toward center field. With your glove arm properly extended out toward the catcher, your body should appear to be in the shape of a big "X" from the view of the third-base coach (assuming you're a right-hander). This is a good check-point when working on your mechanics.

As your arm begins to descend toward the release point, centrifugal force assists in building arm speed. Centrifugal force is the force created by the arm rotating outward or away from the axis (your body). Your hips rotate open and clear a path for your arm to travel. When your arm is parallel to the ground, your wrist is still cocked. Brace your front leg like a strong post, enabling it to accept the forward momentum of your delivery. Keep your palm behind the ball and snap your wrist, releasing the ball just past the hip.

Feel the ball roll off your fingertips as you snap your wrist. This maximizes the forward rotation put on the ball as it travels to home plate. Forward rotation helps the ball sink on its path to the plate. Sinking action causes hitters to swing and miss, or hit the top of the softball. Topped ground balls are easy plays for your infielders.

As the ball is released, explode through the release with your lower body. Use the strength of your rear leg. Continue on that straight line with your armswing. Your arm circle, hip torque, and wrist snap are what generate velocity on your pitches.

Finishing Your Pitch

Your motion is not complete once the pitch is released. You've got to finish the pitch, which is also called the follow-through.

After your wrist snaps and your fingers roll off the ball, continue moving your arm upward. Bend at the elbow and finish with your elbow in front of your face. Your finishing point will vary when throwing different pitches. For example, when throwing a drop-curve, your pitching arm finishes across your pivot leg. The follow-through for fastballs, however, always finishes with your elbow near the height of your chin.

Your pivot foot (the foot that pivots on the pitching rub-

When throwing a fastball, finish by bending at the elbow and your pitching hand raised above your head.

ber) drags forward along the ground after the pitch is released. It pulls forward until it squares up with your plant foot. Dragging the foot forward puts you in good fielding position, should the ball be hit back to you.

DO I ESTABLISH VELOCITY OR ACCURACY?

Coaches often debate whether a young pitcher should maximize her velocity first and then focus on controlling her pitch, or develop control first and work on increasing velocity. The best approach is to master the proper mechanics first, maintain those mechanics while throwing the ball as hard as possible, and then refine your control through repetitious training.

Learning the fundamentals of the windmill delivery builds the best foundation from which a pitcher can improve. Executing the correct mechanics maximizes speed, while keeping the body in balance throughout the motion. It also helps to avoid injury.

By concentrating on accuracy in the early stages, young pitchers tend to hold back and compensate their natural motion by aiming the ball. They don't "let it go," and as a result, fall short of their potential.

While maintaining a sound motion, throw the ball as hard as you can to a large target. Try to throw as many balls as possible to that target, but do so by throwing the ball at maximum effort. Little by little, reduce the size of that target. Eventually, you'll become proficient at throwing strikes with hard fastballs and proper mechanics.

DEVELOPING YOUR PITCHING REPERTOIRE

The fastball is the most important pitch in developing proper mechanics. To pitch with success, you must establish command of your fastball. It's your bread and butter, your "go to" pitch when you have to throw a strike. It's the foundation from which all of your other pitches are born.

At lower levels of play, the fastball is the pitch you use to throw strikes and work ahead in the count. At advanced levels, however, straight pitches are hit a country mile. In order to stay one step ahead of these batters, you've got to develop some other pitches to combat their talents. Pitches such as the drop, change, curve, or rise are tough to hit because they move and travel at different speeds. It's easier to put the sweet spot of the bat on a straight pitch thrown at the same speed. Like Olympic pitcher Lisa Fernandez once said, "In my mind, deception and movement are the keys to a successful pitcher."

Throwing a variety of pitches doesn't just make a hitter's task more difficult physically, but also mentally. Hitters become confused and attempt to guess at what type of pitch may or may not be coming next. Uncertainty works against the hitters, making them somewhat apprehensive and blurring their aggressiveness.

Once you've developed sound mechanics and established good control of your fastball, begin experimenting with new pitches. As you build your repertoire, keep in mind that quality is more important than quantity. It's better to have three or four really good pitch types, rather than six or seven mediocre ones. Uncontrollable factors like body type, hand size, and pitching styles may allow or not allow you to throw certain pitches successfully. Recognize the pitches you throw best through trial and error and go with your strengths.

CREATING MOVEMENT

Fastballs don't necessary have to be straight pitches. In fact, a fastball with movement can be as effective as a change, curve, drop, or rise pitch. Pitches thrown at high velocities with movement are very difficult for hitters to handle.

To create movement on your fastball, apply more pressure to one part of the ball than the other. Accomplish this by pressing down harder with your pointer finger or ring finger. For example, by applying additional pressure with the pointer finger, the ball will travel with a left to right spin upon release. The ball will tail. (A ball that tails means it moves to the side of the pitcher's throwing arm.) By applying more pressure to the ring finger, the ball will cut, which means it moves to the opposite side of the pitcher's throwing arm. The delivery and release of the pitch is identical to the fastball, but the ball moves enough to tie up the hitter.

Change-Up

A good change-up is a devastating pitch for hitters to handle. It's a straight pitch thrown similar to the fastball, but travels at a slower speed. It's an off-speed pitch used to disrupt the hitter's timing.

The reason that change-ups are effective is because they're nearly impossible to detect. The rotation of the ball (in most change-ups) is

Tightening the grip of your fastball and moving the ball back into your palm is the easiest method of throwing a change-up.

the same as a fastball, so the hitter gears up to swing the bat in anticipation of a fastball. When she starts her swing, she soon realizes that the ball has yet to reach the hitting zone. Unfortunately for her, she's recognized this too late. Once the hands start forward, they're difficult to stop. Most hitters slow the bat down and hit the ball with their weight out in front of them, producing weakly hit balls to the infield.

There are several types of change-ups you can throw. The simplest method is tightening the grip on your fastball. Keep your fingers in the same position as you would when throwing a fastball, but squeeze the ball tightly with your fingers. Holding the ball extra tight will reduce the speed of the pitch, which is the primary goal of the change-up.

Another slight alteration is to hold the ball back in your palm. Instead of holding the ball in your fingers as you're supposed to when throwing a fastball, jam it back in your hand. This decreases the velocity of the pitch by minimizing your wrist snap upon release.

More advanced change-ups require a different type of release. Experiment with the circle, the backhand, and the stiff-wristed change-ups. See which type works best for you.

THE CIRCLE CHANGE

This is the easiest of the advanced change-ups to throw if you become comfortable with the grip. Your arm swing and release are identical to your fastball, but the grip is altered to diminish velocity. Lay your pinkie alongside of the ball and tuck your thumb underneath it. Place your three middle fingers on top of the ball across the seams. Apply pressure to the ball only with the thumb and middle fingers. The other fingers should remain limp. The back of the ball should press against your palm when using this grip.

Deliver the ball with the identical motion and wrist snap as you would your fastball. Minimize your follow-through so that your elbow reaches the chest level. The ball is thrown with the same spin as the fastball, making the circle change undetectable to the batter. The circle grip reduces the speed of the pitch and impairs the hitter's timing.

THE STIFF-WRIST CHANGE-UP

To throw a stiff-wristed change-up, use the fastball grip. Your motion remains the same, but when you release the ball, keep your wrist stiff. Do not allow your wrist to propel the ball forward and don't let your fingers roll off the ball. Pretend that your arm, wrist, hand, and fingers are all one piece, with no joints or ability to flex. By not snapping your wrist, the ball travels at a reduced speed.

The only drawback of this type of change-up is that there is very little (if any) spin on the ball. Slower rotation of the seams as the pitch approaches can alert an astute hitter that it's an off-speed pitch. To get a feel for its effectiveness, try the stiff-wrist change-up in practice and use your teammates as guinea pigs. If they're consistently fooled, use it in the game.

THE BACKHANDED CHANGE

The backhanded pitch is a deceptive pitch as well because the grip and motion look similar to those used for the fastball. The difference occurs at the point of release.

Take the same grip you would to throw a fastball. As your arm descends downward and forward in your delivery, turn your wrist so that your hand stays on top of the ball. The back of your hand should face home plate. Do not allow your hand to rotate underneath the ball. Keep your hand on top and flip it out of your hand. Imagine the motion of your wrist when unfolding and spreading a towel on the beach, sheets on a bed, or a tablecloth on a table. With your palm facing down, your wrist snaps forward. This is the same type of motion used for the backhanded change-up.

Shorten your follow-through so that your arm stops about waist-high. If your follow-through is too high, it becomes increasingly difficult to throw the pitch accurately. Most of your pitches will sail high and out of the strike zone.

The backwards spin will alert a good hitter, but you're selling the pitch on your motion. It takes a lot of effort to throw the backhanded change, and exhibiting extreme effort gives the impression of an incoming fastball. Pay attention to how hitters respond to your backhanded change-ups and establish whether it's a pitch worth using.

The Drop Ball

Any pitch that has sink or drop is one that's popular with pitchers. Balls moving downward on their way to the plate induce batters to hit ground balls. Most long balls and extra base hits are batted through the air. Ground balls rarely get pitchers into trouble.

There are two popular types of drop pitches thrown in fast-pitch softball: the peel drop and the turnover drop. Each is unique, but both are effective. Try them both and see which works best for you. You may find that you'll want to add both of them to your repertoire.

THE PEEL DROP

To throw the peel drop, use the standard fastball grip. Start your windmill delivery and execute the mechanics the same as if you were planning to throw your fastball. Using your stride when throwing a fastball as a reference, shorten your stride to throw the peel drop. Lisa Fernandez estimates that the stride she takes when throwing the peel drop is about six inches shorter than the stride she takes for her fastball.

By taking a shorter stride, your weight shifts forward a bit sooner. Your upper body gets out over your front foot and leans forward slightly. This raises and accelerates your point of release. As you prepare to release the pitch, position your hand so it's on the back side of the ball, instead of underneath of it. Raise your shoulder blade (of your pitching arm) slightly just before releasing the ball. Pull up on the ball and snap your wrist forward as you release. Your pitching arm should finish farther out in front of your body, rather than raised over your head.

The increased topspin created by this release forces the ball to drop as it reaches home plate. Practice throwing pitches so that they start in the lower half of the strike zone. Once the ball drops or sinks, it becomes a difficult pitch for batters to drive with authority. Stay away from the upper region of the strike zone. Any type of drop pitch is not meant to be thrown up in the zone. Hitters can do damage to high drop balls.

A photo of the turnover drop grip. Your pointer and middle fingers should lie against the left seam, while your ring finger rests on the right side of the right seam.

TURNOVER DROP

The turnover drop has a special grip and delivery. Hold the ball out in front of you so the seams facing you form a letter U. Place your index and middle finger up against the left seam. Rest your ring finger on the right side of the right seam. Your thumb and pinkie finger slide underneath the ball.

Identical to the mechanics of the peel drop, shorten the

stride in your pitching delivery. As you approach the point of release, raise your pitching shoulder slightly. Turn your hand over as you release the ball so that your middle fingers are rolling over the top of the ball as you let go.

The best time to throw drop pitches is when you're hoping to coax the batter into hitting a ground ball. Perhaps the bases are loaded with one out. A ground ball can set up a double play or force out at the play. A peel drop or turnover drop might be the perfect pitch for this situation.

The Curveball

Curveballs are noted for making batters swing and miss, but they are also very effective when batters make contact. The curve on the ball moves it just enough to miss the sweet spot of the bat. Batters make a lot of outs based on the fact that they got a little jammed (contacted below the sweet spot) or hit the ball just off the end of the bat (contacted above the sweet spot). A ball contacted above or below the sweet spot produces a weakly hit ball, one that your defense can handle with ease.

Also, the marginal change of speed fools hitters, forcing them out onto their front foot as they swing the bat. This produces a weakened swing, which again, results in weak

Because the hand turns over upon release, your pitching hand should face outward in the follow-through.

The curveball grip is similar to the turnover drop. The difference is that your middle finger slides over to press up against the right side of the right seam. This produces more of a sideways rotation.

To generate maximum sideways spin on the ball, finish with your pitching arm across your body, near your hip.

hits easily handled by the defense.

To throw a good curveball, focus on the grip and the follow-through. Following that approach will make the ball break. Once you're getting the ball to break each time you throw a curve, start to establish control of the pitch and work on throwing it to different locations.

To throw a curveball, hold the ball as if you were going to throw a two-seam fastball. Rest your pointer finger against the right side of the left seam, and your middle finger along the right side of the right seam. Your ring and pinkie fingers rest on the right side of the ball, and your thumb is placed underneath the left side of the ball.

As you deliver the pitch, keep your hand underneath the ball with the palm facing up. Turn your hand over the top of the ball as you release the pitch. The motion is similar to turning a doorknob to the left (for right-handed pitchers). Pull your arm across your body on the follow-through. Your palm faces down in the follow-through. The turning of your hand and follow-through gives the ball a sideways spin, which makes the ball curve.

Be smart whenever your throw a curveball. Start it down the middle so it curves outside or inside on a batter. Throw it at a batter so it curves across the inside part of the plate. Never throw it so it curves across the middle of the plate. This is often referred to as a "fat pitch" and can be hit hard and deep.

The Riseball

The riseball is the most sophisticated pitch to throw, but is very effective. Every other pitch thrown in softball either sinks or remains on the same plane. The rise pitch moves upward and befuddles hitters.

To grip a rise pitch, hold the ball so the horseshoe created by the seams faces you. Put your pointer and middle finger on top of the ball.

Slide your pointer finger over to the right so it presses up against the left side of a seam. Rest your middle finger against the left side of the seam. These two fingers nearly connect, with only a seam separating them. Place your thumb on the left side of the ball and tuck your ring and pinkie fingers down on the left side of the ball.

The rise grip is similar to the curve, except pressure is applied to the opposite sides of the seams. Place your pointer finger on the left side of the left seam and middle finger on the left side of the right seam.

Throwing a rise pitch requires you to adjust the mechanics of your delivery. As you're throwing a fastball, your weight shifts forward as you release the pitch. Once the pitch is released, your weight continues forward (although controlled) with the follow-through. When throwing the rise pitch, stay back longer on your rear leg. You want to feel as if you're almost fighting your forward momentum as your arm swings forward. This allows you to cut under the ball and apply backward rotation to the ball. The following steps show how to do it.

Begin to shift your weight forward as your arm circles downward. Instead of having your front leg accept and control the forward weight shift, resist the weight so it stops your forward progress. This is when you "fight gravity." The rear leg collapses slightly, lowering your point of release. Arch your back slightly backward to get your hand under the ball.

With your hips completely closed, your elbow grazes your side as the arm comes through. Lead with your pinkie, snap the ball, and yank up with your arm. Finish with your elbow up in front of your face.

The rise is a good pitch to throw with two strikes. Use it to lure a hitter into swinging at a pitch up and out of the strike zone. To get a called strike, start a riseball down and out off the strike zone, so it breaks up into the lower region of the strike zone. Never throw a rise that breaks into a hitter's wheelhouse.

PITCHING WITH A PURPOSE

Some fortunate pitchers are described as having "great stuff." This means that they possess a deceptive change-up, sharp-breaking curve-

Good pitching requires more than knowing how to throw certain pitches. You've got to understand the who, what, when, where, and why. Work with your catcher to set up hitters.

ball, or a drop pitch that appears to fall off of a table. The most polished pitchers may have all of these. Great stuff, however, can only get you so far. Hitters at advanced levels will eventually catch up to these pitches and challenge your pitching resolve. To become a great pitcher, you've got to know *how* to pitch and use your pitches where they are most effective.

Defining the Role of Your Pitches

Getting the most out of your pitches requires an objective analysis of how each pitch works best for you. Each type of pitch in your arsenal should have its own distinct profile as to how it can be used to get hitters out. Because pitchers come in all different sizes and talent levels, you've got to distinguish how your pitches work for you.

Drop pitches are best used to produce ground balls. Pitches sinking downward are tough to lift and hitters commonly beat them into the ground. Curveballs are best used when hitters are looking for fastballs. They draw hitters off balance and produce swings and misses. Curveballs are also effective when you're ahead in the count and looking for a strikeout.

Maybe your best pitch is the riseball. Perhaps it's your change-up. Whichever pitch is your "go-to" pitch, use it in crucial situations. On 2-2 counts and 3-2 counts, attack the hitter with your best pitch. Don't throw a pitch you're unsure of and get beat with something other than your best.

Setting Up the Hitter

By changing speeds and varying pitch locations, you can set up the hitter. Setting up the hitter means that the pitch thrown to get the hitter out was assisted by the previous pitches thrown during the at bat.

For example, by throwing off-speed pitches to the outside part of the plate, the batter will start to lean out over the plate in anticipation of another outside pitch. Throwing a hard screwball on the inside corner can surprise the hitter in a manner that she's unable to get the barrel on the pitch. Below is a sequence of pitches used to set up the hitter.

Curveball on the outside corner—strike one; 0-1 count
Peel drop low—ball one; 1-1 count
Curveball outside corner—fouled off for strike two; 1-2 count
Curveball outside and low—ball two; 2-2 count
Screwball inside corner—called strike three; you're out!

Because the batter was fed a steady diet of off-speed pitches on the outside part of the plate, her eyes become fixed on slower pitches that are away from her. By buzzing a screwball on the inside corner, she'll have trouble reacting in time to hit the ball solid. At times, she may even freeze and take a called third strike. Pitching is more than throwing hard and being equipped with a full arsenal of different pitches. It also entails observation and strategic planning.

EXPOSING WEAKNESSES

Each batter has her own individual batting stance, but certain characteristics of a batting stance can unveil weaknesses in a hitter and factor into your plan of attack.

Hands held high—difficulty handling low strikes and hard pitches thrown inside

Hands held low—difficulty handing high strikes, riseballs

Excessive movement in the stance—difficulty staying back on off-speed pitches

Closed stance—difficulty handling hard pitches inside

Open stance—trouble handling pitches on the outside part of the plate

No flex in the knees—trouble hitting low strikes

Wide stance—trouble hitting hard pitches inside and riseballs

Narrow stance—difficulty handling off-speed pitches

Slap hitter—pitch her down and inside

Power hitter—pitch her down and outside

FIELDING THE PITCHER'S POSITION

Pitching is your main focus on the mound, but once the ball is released, you become another infielder. The pitcher has responsibilities on the field much like a second baseman or center fielder. Play your position adequately and you can help get yourself back in the dugout and up to bat.

After your follow-through is complete, jump into the fielder's position. Spread your feet, flex your knees, and bend at the waist. If the ball is hit to you, field the ball with two hands, step to your target, and make a firm throw to the base. Because you're very close to the batter, the ball will arrive quickly. Take your time and set your feet. You may have to wait a second or two for the baseman to arrive at the bag.

Always know what you're going to do with the ball before it's hit to you. Know the game situation—inning, score, number of outs, runners on base, speed of the base runners—and decide where you're going with the ball before it's hit to you. Where you throw the ball may vary by where the ball is hit. For example, with a runner on first base and nobody out, there is a force play at first and second base. If the ball is hit directly back to you, turn and throw to second base for the lead runner and possible double play. If the ball is hit slowly to your right or left, throw to first base and take the sure out.

Backing Up Bases

Batted balls to the outfield require throws to an infield base. It's your responsibility to back up bases in these situations. Long, hard throws from the outfield can be difficult to handle and sometimes skip past infielders.

When backing up a base, allow for enough distance between yourself and your teammate to react to a poor throw. Don't stand four feet behind the baseman. You'll have little or no chance to stop an errant throw. Stand at least 10–15 feet behind your teammate. This puts you in good position to stop any high, wide or wildly low throws. Stopping the throw keeps base runners from advancing.

It's essential that you back up all throws to third base and home plate. It's your job to quickly assess which base the ball is being thrown to and at what angle to back up your teammate. Some decisions are impossible to anticipate and must be made on the spot. For example, with runners on first and second and a base hit to the outfield, the outfielder may go for the runner trying to score from second base, or the runner trying to reach third from first base. In this case, sprint to the midpoint of the third base foul line. Turn and see where

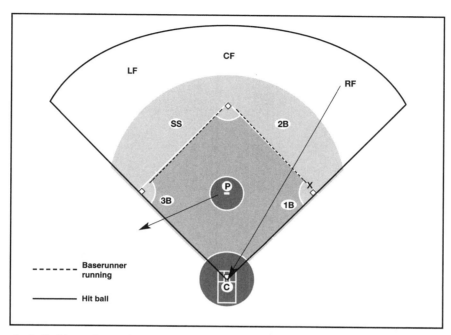

On balls hit to the outfield, the pitcher moves off the mound to back up a throw from the outfielder. In this case, the runner may try to advance to third base, so the pitcher runs behind the third base bag.

the outfielder is directing her throw and then sprint to back up your teammate. Do whatever it takes to stop the ball from getting past you. Receive it like an infielder, drop to one knee or slide, and lay your body out in front of the ball. Just make sure that ball doesn't get past you.

DRILLS

Snap Drill

Snapping your wrist forward upon release adds velocity and movement to your pitches. A stronger wrist snap produces more favorable results. Stand facing your partner who is approximately 10 feet away. With your throwing hand down by your side, take your wrist back slightly and flip the ball to your teammate. Generate as much power as possible with each flip. Snap the ball back and forth 25 times. Practice this drill to increase wrist strength and velocity. Use this drill before warming up to pitch as well.

Practice the snap drill to strengthen your wrist and increase velocity and movement to your pitches.

Two for One

Take two balls out on the field. Give one to your catcher and keep one for yourself. Take the mound and set up to throw pitches to home plate. As you deliver a pitch to the plate, the catcher fires a ground ball back at you. Field the ball, and use it for your next pitch. Continue this routine until you've thrown 20 pitches. This drill quickens your reaction time and gets you into the habit of preparing for balls hit back to the mound.

Pitching for Distance

This drill builds arm strength, but still forces the pitcher to concentrate on throwing balls accurately.

With a catcher at home plate, stand 20 feet away and pitch the ball to the catcher. Once you've thrown five strikes (the catcher is the judge) move back 10 feet. Pitch balls from 30 feet away until you've thrown five strikes and then move back another 10 feet. Continue doing this until you've reached 60 feet. Throwing from distances longer than 43 feet stretches your arm out and builds up arm strength. Try to complete all the intervals in the least amount of pitches.

Patriot Games

Make a home plate out of white cardboard or poster paper. Divide the plate into three equal regions. Color the left region red, leave the middle region white, and color the right region blue.

Using your homemade plate, throw ten pitches to the catcher. Award yourself two points for every pitch that crosses over the red and blue

Pitching from increased distances increases arm strength. Practice this drill regularly.

regions, and one point for each pitch that crosses over the white region. Pitches traveling off the plate receive zero points. For bonus points, you can call your shot. Any called pitch over the red or blue region is worth three points. Collect the most possible points after ten pitches.

Isolation Drill

This drill isolates the final stage of the pitching motion. With a teammate positioned approximately 30 feet away, stand with your feet aligned to your partner. Raise your pitching arm up and curl it above your head so it replicates the letter "C." From this position, swing your arm down, fire your hips, and throw a pitch to your teammate. This drill isolates the latter portion of the delivery, allowing you to concentrate on those specific elements of the pitching motion.

Walk Up and Chuck

Weight shift is essential to maximizing the velocity of your fastballs. The Walk Up and Chuck drill gives pitchers an idea of what the proper weight shift feels like.

Stand with a ball approximately six to eight feet behind the pitching rubber. Without breaking stride, walk forward, step on the rubber, break into your windmill delivery, and throw. The momentum that is

Perfecting your mechanics can be accomplished by breaking the pitching motion into pieces. This drill isolates the final stage of the pitching motion.

built up as you approach the rubber and is maintained through the delivery gives you a genuine feel of what the forward weight shift should feel like in your pitching motion.

This drill may take a few tries to find the right distance and correct sequence of steps, but the important point is to step on the rubber without breaking the momentum of your approach.

Below the Knees

During pitching practice, take your final 15 pitches and challenge your teammates to a pitching accuracy competition. With your catcher set up in her customary stance, target the area from her kneecaps down to her feet. Any ball (throw over the plate) that is caught or below the catcher's knees without touching the ground is worth a point. Compete to see who can accumulate the most points in their final 15 pitches.

One bonus point is awarded to any pitch thrown in the scoring area that is not a fastball. Curves, drops, change-ups, screwballs, etc. are all worth two points.

This drill trains pitchers to throw the ball down in or below the strike zone, but not wildly low. Low pitches are tougher pitches to drive for power.

6

BASERUNNING

Running the bases in softball is an undervalued skill. Efficient baserunning can win games, while inefficient baserunning can lose games. Hitting, pitching, and defense certainly hold their merit, but baserunning is a facet of the game often overlooked by coaches and players. To score, you've got to circle the bases without fault. Make a mistake on the basepaths and it can prove costly.

To many, a good base runner is a player who runs fast. This is an inaccurate assumption. There are players with great speed who are poor base runners, and those with average speed who excel on the basepaths. Speed can aid a base runner, but it's not required for proficiency.

All good base runners possess two characteristics. They are *aggressive* and they are *intelligent*. If you run the bases aggressively, instinctively, and with an awareness of the surrounding factors, you'll be a threat to score each time you reach base.

AGGRESSIVE BASERUNNING

When you're on base, the goal is very simple: get to the next base. Do not become complacent standing on first base, second base, or third base. The only time your team receives any credit is when you reach home plate. Seize any opportunity that allows you to advance to the next base.

What does it mean to be aggressive? It means rounding each base with fervor, looking for a defensive player to bobble the ball or make

Running the bases efficiently can lead to more hits, runs, and victories.

an errant throw. It means scoring from second base on a base hit to right field, because you know that the right fielder is playing deep and has a weak arm. It means challenging the defense to make a play by stretching a single into a double when the chances of making it safely are fifty-fifty. Remember, for a player to throw you out, several steps must fall perfectly in line. The outfielder must field the ball and throw it accurately. The receiving player must be in the proper position over the bag, field the ball cleanly, and apply an efficient tag. If any one of those steps in the process breaks down, you'll slide in safely.

There are times in the game when it's good to be aggressive and other times to run the bases conservatively. Be aggressive early in the game. Taking the lead in a game is important. If the game is tied in the late innings, it pays to be aggressive. Late-game jitters often disrupt the defense's execution. It's up to you to take advantage. Lastly, if you're ahead by a small margin late in the game, be aggressive at all times. Drive the nail in the opposition's coffin and win the game. Taking an extra base can provide an important insurance run, and as a result, deflate the spirit of your opponent.

Taking unnecessary risks when you're losing a game is ill-advised. If you're down by several runs, getting runners on base is critical. Don't jeopardize your team's chances of a big-inning rally. Think about running from base to base and look to your base coaches for guidance.

Trailing late in the game by more than one run is also a time to be conservative. By reaching base, you've given your team a spark. Rely on your hitters to advance you and eventually drive you home.

WHEN TO BE AGGRESSIVE

- Early innings of a close game.
- Any time the score is tied.
- When the defense looks shaky or out of position.
- Late in the game when you're ahead by a small margin.
- Late in the game when you're behind by one run (with intelligence).

WHEN TO STAY CONSERVATIVE

- Trailing by more than one run early in the game.
- Behind by more than one run late in the game.
- Ahead by a large number of runs (a blow-out).

SMART BASERUNNING

As mentioned, the second part of being a good base runner is intelligence. Aggressiveness is only a positive attribute if it's combined with sensibility. Anyone can run around the bases with reckless abandon. It takes intuitiveness and observation to understand when to "turn the jets on."

Like a hitter observing a pitcher during a pre-game warm-up, it's a good idea to watch the opposition take infield/outfield practice before the game. Find out which outfielders have strong, fair, or weak arms. What is their mobility like when running for balls hit to their right or left? How accurate are their throws? This information can prove invaluable during the game. If you notice the left fielder has a weak arm and then hit a ball down the third baseline, you know you've got a great chance of stretching a single into a double.

Another element to pay attention to is positioning. Are the outfielders playing deep? If you're on first base and the rightfielder is playing very deep, you can advance to third base on a single to right field. Are the outfielders playing shallow? If so, when a ball is hit to a deep part of the park, you won't have to wait to see if the outfielder catches it. You'll know the ball will carry over her head and can start running immediately.

Neglecting to back up bases on throws and failing to correctly cover bases are mistakes defense players frequently make. By being attentive, you can make them pay for their flaws and take the extra base.

RUNNING TO FIRST BASE

Becoming a good base runner begins right from the start. Once you put the ball in play, you've made the transition from hitter to base runner. Getting a good jump out of the batter's box is the difference between an out and an infield single, a single and a double, a double and a triple. On a larger scale, it could mean the difference between a win and a loss.

Note: Before discussing your jump out of the batter's box, understand that running to first begins after *you've completed your swing. Do not cut your swing short in an effort to dash to first base sooner. You'll sacrifice power and consistency at the plate by doing so. Finish your swing and then make your move toward first base.*

To get a good jump out of the batter's box, use your upper and lower body. For a right-handed batter, drive your right arm forward and push off your left leg. (Lefties should drive the left arm and push off with the right leg.) Square your hips and shoulders to the base and begin running. Sprint down the baseline at top speed.

Your first steps out of the box should be explosive. Your first three steps are low and explosive. Do not stand up and then run. Push off the balls of your feet. Keep your head up and arms pumping. Run on direct line to the bag at full

Right-handed batters should drive their right arm forward and push off their left leg.

speed. Keep your body relaxed and tension-free. Make sure you breathe, inhaling and exhaling as you run down the line. Straining to create more speed will slow you down. Stay loose and relaxed running straight through the bag.

It's a good idea to imagine that the finish line is about four feet past the base. That way, you'll avoid slowing down as you approach the base. Remember—run *through* the bag, not *to* the bag.

Don't Peek

Runners are often guilty of peeking at the infield as they run to first base. They're interested to see if the ball makes it through to the infield, or if the infielder might be late in throwing the ball to first base. This is a no-no. After you put the ball in play, focus only on running to first base. You can neither control what the fielder does nor should you care. Run to first base as swiftly as you can. If the ball goes through to the outfield, your first-base coach will tell you to make a turn toward second base.

If you're a "peeker," ask yourself this question: Have you ever seen a world-class sprinter like Marion Jones or Gail Devers turn her head while running a track race? It's very doubtful. That's because it slows you down. Turning your head to focus on an infielder takes your attention off your sole purpose, which is getting to first base. The slightest deviation from that focus slows you down.

After you run through the bag, turn to face the infield. Prepare yourself to continue on to second base if the ball is overthrown. If not, return to first base in foul territory.

Approaching the Base

Watching the finish of an Olympic track race is very exciting. Commonly, a pack of runners crosses the finish within hundredths of a second of each other. Visualize that image—runners finishing in full-stride, chest out, arms pumping. Your finish should be no different. Do not lunge, do not jump, and do not slide. These methods slow you down as you approach the base and also may cause injury.

The only time to consider altering your path to first base is if the throw pulls the first baseman off the bag. If the throw is to the first baseman's left, she'll try to catch the ball and tag you. To avoid a tag, slide or move outward to the foul territory side of the base. Tag the base with your left foot and spin away from the field. If the throw is high and the first baseman is forced to jump to the foul territory side, move toward the infield side of the base or slide so she can't tag you on the head.

MAKING TURNS

Stroking a base hit to the outfield is a great feeling. But the time to celebrate a hit is after the game with mom and dad. Remember, once the ball leaves the bat, you're no longer a hitter, you're a base runner. The object is now to get to the next base. Make a strong turn towards second base. It's the sign of a player who knows how to run the bases and is ready to take advantage of outfield error.

On a base hit to the outfield, don't sprint straight down the first baseline. Instead, "bow out" toward foul territory in preparation of making a turn toward second base (*see photo*). After taking your first few steps out of the box, curve your run to the right of the foul line. By the time you're two-thirds of the way to first base, you should be approximately five feet off the foul line. Now begin to curve back to first base so that you can hit the bag and continue running on a straight line to second base.

The reason you bow out is to maintain your momentum as you advance to second base. If you were to run straight to first base, you'd have to slow to a near stop, turn toward second base, and then start running again. This is not an efficient method of baserunning. Make a

(This page and next) Once you see that the ball has made it past the infield, bow out to the right and make a gradual turn as you approach first base (above). Step on the corner of the base and push off towards second base. It's preferable to hit the base with your left foot, but the important thing is to hit the base at full speed, without breaking stride.

gradual turn outward, then turn back inward, and hit the bag running full steam toward second base.

On base hits, stop about one-third of the way to second base. Make sure it's an aggressive turn. The outfielder might bobble the ball or it may get past them. In this case, continue running to second base. Making an aggressive turn can also coax an outfielder into rushing a throw to second base. An errant throw may also allow you to advance.

By failing to make an aggressive turn, you have left no chance of reaching second base. Do not become content just because you just got a hit. Make sure you're in position to take advantage if an opportunity presents itself.

Minimizing Angles

Baserunning is not only about speed, but minimizing angles and maintaining momentum. Making wide turns or slowing down on approaching bases increases the time it takes for you to get from point A to point B. Run the bases efficiently and umpires will be calling you "Safe!" regularly.

On plays where you're attempting to advance two bases, turn outward approximately halfway to the base. Starting your turn early minimizes the depth of your turn, and allows you to maintain momentum rounding the base. As you near the base, lean inward (to the left) with your left shoulder. Touch the bag with whichever foot comes up first.

(It's best to hit the bag with your left foot, but not at the expense of slowing down or stutter-stepping just to make sure the left foot hits the bag.) Step on the inside corner of the base, which enables you to push off the base in the direction of the next base. Stepping on top of the base is fruitless. You can't push off the top of the base.

Once you've touched the base, continue leaning inward until your upper and lower body are square to the next base. When your legs get underneath you, continue sprinting at top speed.

Employ this method any time you're running for extra bases. Whether you've smacked a double or triple, are running from first to third on a batted ball, or are attempting to score from second base on a single, cut angles and use your body weight to reduce your running time. Tighten up your turns to shorten the distance covered along the base paths, but don't cut your turns so close that you're unable to maintain momentum.

As you approach second base, look up at the third-base coach. If she's waving you on to advance to third base, continue running without breaking stride. Make sure you pick up on the third-base coach's instructions early enough so you can make a strong turn toward third base if she's waving you on.

Leaning in with your left shoulder as you touch first base helps steer your momentum toward second base.

When taking your lead, always anticipate advancing to the next base. Good base runners are aggressive base runners.

After the pitch is released, take approximately three steps and face the hitter. Look in to home plate to see if the ball is hit, taken, or gets past the catcher.

LEADS

Aggressive leads help runners take extra bases, beat force plays, and advance on a passed ball or wild pitch. Timid leads leave runners stranded on base. Much like a track runner, a good start can make all the difference.

Leads Off First Base

When leading off first base, place your left foot on the front corner or side of the bag. Place your right foot behind the base in foul territory. Use a rocker step (momentum builder) and as the pitcher begins wind-up, simply rock back onto your rear leg. When the pitcher reaches the top of her circle, drive the right foot forward. This allows the left foot to push off as the pitcher releases the ball. Take three low and explosive strides towards second base (appear as though stealing second). Stay balanced in your lead and turn your body to face the pitcher, ready to either advance or get back to the base.

GETTING BACK TO THE BASE

More often than not, balls are not put in play by the batter. Pitches are thrown out of the strike zone, taken, or missed by the hitter. The catcher ends up with the ball, and is capable of snapping a throw to first base. Stay alert and get back to the base as soon as you see contact is not made.

As you shuffle off the base, keep your weight on the balls of your feet. Pause, in a balanced position, as the ball crosses home plate. To return to first base, use a crossover step (right over left) to square up with the bag. If there is no throw from the catcher, run two or three more steps back to the base. Always run toward the back of the base. Return to the base standing up, and prepare to take your lead for the next pitch.

If the catcher throws down to first, take the same first step; cross over with the right foot. Stay low (in a crouched position) and dive back to the base headfirst. Dive toward the back of first base and extend your right arm. As you hit the ground, turn your head toward the outfield. This protects your face in case a low throw gets past the first baseman.

REACTING FROM FIRST BASE

Situation: Runner on first base—less than two outs

Ground ball	*Run to second base as hard as you can; slide*
Line drive	*Freeze; run back if it's caught, advance if it goes through*
Fly ball	*Run halfway to second base; await the results*
Base hit	*Run to second, look to advance to third base*
Extra base hit	*Run to third base, look to score*
Wild pitch/ passed ball	*Advance to second base*
Pitch in the dirt	*Look to advance to second base*
Fly ball in foul territory	*Run back to the base and look to tag up on the play*
Bunt	*Run to second base*
Home run	*Touch 'em all*

Situation: Runner on first base—two outs

Ground ball	*Running on contact*
Line drive	*Running on contact*
Fly ball	*Running on contact*
Base hit	*Run to second base; look to advance to third base*
Extra base hit	*Look to score*
Wild pitch/ passed ball	*Advance to second base*
Pitch in the dirt	*Look to advance to second base*
Fly ball in foul territory	*Running on contact*
Home run	*Touch 'em all*

Always reach for the back of first base with your right hand. This affords you a little more time to get back safely, because the first baseman will have to reach back to apply the tag. If you dive toward the front of first base, the tag is much easier to administer.

Another method of getting back to the base without diving is to cross over with your right foot, extend to the back of the base with your left foot, then open your body to the field by pivoting on your left foot. Your right leg swings open like a gate and the right foot lands in foul territory. This increases the distance between you and the first baseman applying the tag and also puts you in position to advance on an errant throw.

When diving back to first base on a throw from the catcher, reach for the back of the base with your right arm.

Leads Off Second Base

On second base, take a bigger lead. Assume the same lead position described on first base. As the pitch is released, cross over the base with your right leg and run three or four steps toward third base, and then turn your body to face the hitter. Your goal is to score on a base hit, so cut some distance down by taking an aggressive lead. If the pitch is taken, run back to second base. The shortstop or second baseman may sneak in behind you to take a throw from the catcher. The last thing you want is to get picked off.

On ground balls hit to your left (meaning anything hit to the left side of where you're positioned), advance to third base. If the ball is hit on the ground to your right, hold your ground and shuffle back to second base. On base hits, make a turn on your way to third, assuming you're going to score. Then, simply listen to the instructions given by your third-base coach. On routine fly balls to left, run halfway to third, and react to the result of the play. On routine fly balls to center and right field, run back to second base and look to tag up. If the ball is hit in the gap or over the outfielder's head, make sure you touch third on your way to scoring a run.

Leads Off Third Base

You're almost home, so be sure you are ready to take off at any instant. Taking the same lead as you did at second base, cross over and run two or three steps toward home plate upon the pitcher's release. Face the batter to witness the result of the pitch.

The defense will dictate how you react to a batted ball. If the defense is playing back, take off for home as soon as you see the ball is hit on the ground. If the first or third baseman is playing up, only run on balls hit to the shortstop or second baseman.

If the infield is playing up, only run home if the ball travels through the infield and into the outfield. Freeze on line drives and run back to the base and tag on fly balls to the outfield. With two outs, run on contact.

Passed balls and wild pitches occur frequently at amateur levels. Be on the balls of your feet, ready to take advantage if this happens. It's an easy way to score a run. Take into consideration how far the backstop sits from the catcher. If it's very close, it may be too risky to try and score. If it's deep, race home as soon as you see the ball get past the catcher.

STEALING BASES

The art of stealing a base is very simple. As the pitcher releases the ball, run as fast as you can to the next base. If you beat the throw from the catcher, you're sliding in safely.

There are some do's and don'ts that can improve your stealing technique. The entire play, from the pitcher's release to the infielder receiving the throw at the base, only takes a few seconds. Any time you can save a few hundredths of a second here or there will improve your success rate.

Stealing Second Base

When stealing from first base, assume your customary lead position. Flex at the knees and crouch down a bit. Hold your left arm out in front of you and bend at the elbow so it forms a 90-degree angle with your forearm. Extend your right arm behind you, slightly flexed. Make sure your shoulders and hips are square to second base. Lastly, feel the edge of the base pressed against the ball of your left foot.

As the pitcher releases the pitch, thrust forward by pushing off the base with your left leg. Pump your right arm forward and stride out with your right leg. Remain bent at the waist during your initial movement off the base. Runners often make the mistake of "standing up" first and then running forward. This wastes time. Stay down and move forward.

When stealing a base, don't stand straight up out of your lead. Push off the base and stay low to the ground.

PEEK IN TO HOME PLATE

After your first three or four strides, peek in toward home plate. See what happens on the pitch. The ball might be hit, missed or get past the catcher. React to the situation accordingly.

If the batter takes or misses the pitch, quickly focus on second base. The catcher is trying to gun you down. When you get to about 10 feet from the base, break into your slide. (Sliding will be covered later in this chapter.) Keep your foot (or hand) on the base and ask for time-out. Never lose contact with the base when rising to your feet.

If the ball is hit in the air, stop running. On a ball hit to the out-field, remain halfway between the bases and watch to see if the out-fielder makes the catch. If she does, retreat back to first base. When the ball is popped up to the infield, immediately put on the breaks and sprint back to first base.

On base hits and extra base hits, keep on chugging. You might even be able to score. The important thing to remember is to look into home when you steal. It lets you know what happens on the pitch.

Stealing Third Base

Stealing third base is really no different than stealing second base. The third baseman often has difficulty getting into position to cover the base in time, so be ready if the ball gets past the third base-man on the throw. If it scoots into the outfield, quickly get up and run home.

A FRESH LOOK OFF FIRST BASE

Recently, some base runners have used a slightly different method of leading off first base. Instead of placing their right foot behind first base in foul territory, they place it in front of the left foot in fair territory. The left foot remains against the base, but the front foot is set on the infield side pointing toward second base.

At first glance, this new lead makes perfect sense. You're starting closer to second base, so why wouldn't it be used all the time?

This lead has not been popular in the past, because runners are often called out for leaving the base before the pitcher releases the ball. Also, even though their right foot starts closer to second base, they have no momentum moving in that direction. They leave the base from a dead standstill.

When the lead is taken from the standard position, the right foot crosses over as the pitcher is delivering the ball. As long as the left foot remains on the base until the pitch is released, the body can begin moving toward second base. So if a good runner times her lead perfectly, her right foot is planting down in fair territory as the pitch is released. Now, the left foot leaves the base and crosses over with momentum moving toward second base.

The new method can work well with good timing, but it's risky. Leave a split-second early and the umpire can call you out.

SLIDING

Sliding is a critical element to good baserunning. It can also be a lot of fun. Sliding allows you to run at top speed into the base and hold it without slowing down. If you don't slide, one of two things will happen. You'll either run past the bag because you're moving too fast to decel-erate in time. In this case, you'll "run" the risk of being tagged out. The other alternative is that you'll slow down as you approach the base to stop your momentum and hold the bag. Neither method is safe or effi-cient. Learn to slide and become a tougher out on the base paths.

There are various sliding techniques used by base runners. Start out learning feet-first slides, because they are the easiest and safest to learn. There are three common types of feet-first slides: bent-leg, hook slide, and the fake hook slide. Each is useful and can be used in certain situations.

A slide should begin approximately 10 feet from the base. To slide feet-first, start by leaning back and throwing your arms and hands up in the air. This protects you from spraining your hands and wrists, a common injury suffered when sliding. Leave your feet and land on your bottom with your feet reaching forward and body leaning backward.

The Bent-Leg Slide

A bent-leg slide is when one leg is bent under the other. The bent leg takes the weight of the slide while the other leg reaches outward for the base. Point the toes of the outstretched foot to the base. After sliding in safely, request a time-out from the umpire so you can stand up and dust off.

When using the bent-leg slide, you can use the firm prop of the base to stand up quickly should the ball escape the fielder and carry into the outfield. This is called a pop-up slide. As the lead foot makes contact with the base, push off the ground with your bent-leg foot. Stand up, find the ball, and if it's safe, advance to the next base.

Proper technique calls for your arms to be raised in the air as you slide. This prevents injury to the hands and wrists.

For the pop-up slide, keep your upper body slightly upright and slide into the bag a little later. Use the base to "pop" yourself up and (possibly) continue running.

The Hook Slide

Another type of slide is a hook slide. This is used when you're trying to avoid a tag. As you're approaching the base, if you notice the fielder is moving to one side of the base to catch the ball, try a hook slide.

This slide begins a bit later than the bent-leg slide. When you notice the fielder is positioned on one side of the base, target your approach to the opposite side. Slide alongside the base (away from the fielder) and bend your leg closest to the base at the knee. Hook your toe on the corner of the base as you pass by. Find the umpire and immediately call time-out.

The Fake Hook Slide

Last is the fake hook slide. Use this slide when the ball (and fielder's glove) gets to the base before you do. If the fielder is positioned on the infield side of the base, slide to the outfield side (and vice-versa). Wait until you're three or four feet from the base and slide past it with both feet. Roll over on your stomach (toward the base) and reach for the back of the base (*see photos*). You might catch the fielder off-guard and avoid the tag.

Run to the side of the base opposite the defensive player. As you reach the base, slide, then roll over and reach out for the base with your opposite-side arm (as shown). This is a great slide to use if the ball beats you to the base but the defensive player is out of position.

Head-First Slides

As you progress and advance to higher levels of play, you may want to try the head-first slide. When executed correctly, this can be the quickest way to slide into a base, especially when stealing. Head-first slides, however, can cause injury.

To slide headfirst, dive outward and downward to the base with your hands and arms outstretched. When hitting the ground, allow your forearms to take the brunt of the fall and reach for the base with your fingertips.

Much like the hook slide and fake hook slide, the head-first slide can be used to avoid a tag. If the ball beats you to the base, dive to the side of the bag opposite of which the fielder stands. As you slide past the base, reach out with the arm closest to the bag and grab it.

DRILLS

The Three-Round Bout

Here is a drill that practices baserunning, but also can double as your conditioning workout.

ROUND 1

Have all the players form a single-file line at home plate. Each player will run to first base as if they hit a ground ball to the infield. (Once a player gets about halfway down the line, the next player in line can start.) All players remain at first base. Next, they get into the lead position on first base and steal second. Make sure the players all remember to look in toward home plate. From second base, players run to third and continue home as if they're scoring on a base hit to the outfield. Make sure they bow out and start their turn toward home plate as they approach third base.

ROUND 2

Have all the players form a single-file line at home plate. One by one, players take off for first base as if they knocked a base hit to the outfield. Each player should bow out and make a strong turn toward second base. From first base, they then take a few shuffle steps and run all the way to third base. On third, they take their lead, walk off, and then run back to the base to tag up. The coach then yells, "Break!" as if the ball has been caught and the runner sprints home.

ROUND 3

From home plate, each player takes off as if they've hit a sure double (a hit to the gap). As they run into second base, they should slide as if it's a close play. Next, each base runner sprints to third base and rounds the bag with the intention of scoring, but the base coach holds them up and they must retreat back to third base. Taking a lead from third, the players slowly walk off third base and then sprint for home plate, as if a ground ball were hit to the infield.

Home Run Relay Race

Here is a conditioning drill that is fun, and allows players to practice running the bases. Split the team into two even groups. Place one group at second base and the other group at home plate. The teams are to run a relay race.

The team standing at second base will take off for third base and continue on to home plate, first base, and then return to second base. When the first runner reaches second base, she slaps the hand of the next runner, who then continues the race. The team from home plate runs the bases in standard fashion (from home to first, second, third, and then back home). The runner then slaps the hand of her teammate standing at home plate, who continues the race.

The team that completes circling the bases first, wins.

The home run relay race is a fun way to practice running the bases. One team starts at home plate (this page) and the other at second base (next page). Circle the bases and hand the ball off to your teammate when you return to your starting point. The first team finished wins the race.

Catch the Crook

Running in softball requires short bursts of speed. The distance between bases is only 60 feet, so getting up to full speed quickly is critical. Catch the Crook develops quickness and speed.

Set up a cone in right field (or left field) that is 40 yards from the foul line. Players partner up with a teammate who has a similar run-

Catch the Crook is an enjoyable way to develop explosiveness. If you're the crook (seated in front), get up and go so that cop doesn't catch you.

ning speed. One player stands on the foul line in the lead position. She is the cop. The other sits on the ground Indian style with her hands flat on the ground to her sides. She is the crook. The crook is positioned 10 feet in front of the cop.

On the coach's signal, the cop and crook take off. The crook gets up as quickly as possible and runs for the cone. The cop tries to catch up to the crook and tag her before she reaches the cone. If the crook makes it to the cone without being touched, she escapes the wrath of the law.

Players jog back to the line and switch places.

Who's the Egg Head?

Dress players in old pairs of pants. This drill is going to produce some grass stains. Take a hose and wet down a 10-foot area in the outfield. Place cones in the outfield that will indicate where the wet grass begins and ends. Put a flat base or softball glove on the ground to give the players a destination to slide to. Line the players up so that they have to run approximately 30 feet to 40 feet before reaching the wet grass.

As the runner prepares to run, hand her two eggs. She must hold the eggs in her hands from the time she starts running straight through the slide. The object is to execute the slide without breaking an egg. If the runner allows her hands to contact the ground during the slide, the eggs will break. If she correctly throws her hands up in the air, the eggs will be safe. On the call of the coach, the runner sprints toward the wet grass and slides feet first. Each player should slide four to six times.

To make this a game, divide the players into two teams. Give each team two eggs. One by one, players take off for the base and slide in hard. The team that goes the longest without breaking both eggs wins.

7

OFFENSIVE STRATEGY

Fast-pitch softball is dominated by pitching and defense. A team who has an outstanding pitcher on the mound has a legitimate chance of beating anybody. Put Lisa Fernandez or Christa Williams on a high school team and any college team will struggle mightily to come out on top.

Because runs are at such a premium in fast-pitch softball, teams must do whatever it takes to manufacture runs. You can't always wait around for three straight doubles or a three-run homer to put runs on the scoreboard. Sometimes, offensive softball necessitates some creative strategy from the bench to push the runs across home plate.

This chapter discusses methods of advancing base runners and how to manufacture runs. Topics like bunting, slap-hitting, and hitting behind runners (hitting a ball that is to the right side of second base while second base is occupied) will be reviewed in theory and execution. Being a solid offensive player entails more than simply putting the bat on the ball. It often means putting the team before your individual desires and approaching home plate with a purpose. At times you'll be asked to bunt, slap-hit, hit and run or try to hit a fly ball. It's in your best interest to master all of these traits; to be the best offensive player you can be.

BUNTING

Bunting is an essential ingredient to an offense in fast-pitch softball. It can be used to get runners on base (drag or push bunt), advance runners on base (sacrifice bunt), or score runners (squeeze bunt). It is a

Bunting, slap hitting, and situational hitting are important methods of manufacturing runs in fast-pitch softball.

trait that can be easily mastered through practice and concentration, but its execution should never be underestimated. Anyone can become a good bunter. Good bunters are born from repetitious training, not inborn talent.

Sacrifice Bunting

Before discussing the fundamentals of bunting, take note of the term "sacrifice bunting." It is titled "sacrifice" because you are sacrificing your at bat to advance a teammate who has already reached base. For example, imagine you're playing a game and it's a tie score in the last inning. The first batter for your team hits a double. She's standing on second base with nobody out. For her to score would require either a single (with a fast runner on second base) or an extra base hit. The other option is to have the hitter sacrifice bunt. By bunting the ball toward first or third base, the hitter will more than likely be thrown out at first base, but the base runner is now standing on third base with one out. She can now score on a base hit, fly ball to the outfield, wild pitch, or even a ground ball to the infield. The chances of taking the lead and winning have increased dramatically.

There are two methods by which you can bunt the ball. You can "square around" or "pivot." Each method is adequate when executed correctly, so it's a matter of personal preference. Beginners commonly use squaring around, so we'll discuss that method first.

SQUARING AROUND— THE SETUP

Any time you bunt the ball, start in your customary batting stance. Move up to the front of the batter's box. This helps keep your bunts in fair territory and also defends against breaking pitches. (If you're up in the box, you'll catch the ball before it breaks.) As the pitcher begins her wind-up, take your rear foot and place it as close to home plate as possible. Your toes should point out toward the pitcher. Turn your front foot so it faces the pitcher and place it approximately shoulder-width apart. Your entire body is now facing the pitcher, knees flexed and slightly bent at the waist (*see photo*).

Note: Be sure not to step on home plate or out of the batter's box when squaring around. If you make contact with the ball from this position, the umpire will rule you out.

PIVOTING—THE SETUP

Pivoting is an easier set-up, but young hitters often fail to cover the outside part of the plate. If you can use the pivot method without making this common mistake, you may find it simpler to employ.

When squaring around to bunt, face the pitcher and flex your knees. Push the bat out in front of you so you can see the ball hit your bat.

When using the pivot method, start closer to home plate to achieve full plate coverage.

Starting from your standard batting stance, move closer to the plate and move up in the batter's box. Pivot both your front and rear feet forward and rotate your hips to face the pitcher. Bend at the knees and face the pitcher with both eyes (*see photo*). It is essential that you move closer to the plate when using the pivot method. If you stand off the plate, you won't reach outside strikes once you pivot.

HOLDING THE BAT

Starting from your normal grip, slide your top hand up to the fat part of the barrel. Hold the bat with your fingers as if you were pinching it with your thumb and pointer finger. Your last three fingers should lay behind the barrel for additional support. Make sure your fingers remain behind the barrel and don't wrap around in front. If you do this, you're putting your fingers in danger of being hit by the ball. Your bottom hand simply slides up to the top of the handle.

Extend your arms out in front of home plate and then pull them back slightly so they're relaxed. Holding the bat out in front allows your eyes to track the ball into your bat. Think of a marksman aiming their rifle. They don't hold the rifle in close toward their body, they hold it out in front of them to improve hand-to-eye coordination.

Hold the bat at the top of the strike zone. That way, anything above your barrel is a ball. Pull the bat back and take the pitch for a ball.

Hold the bat so it's angled upward, making sure balls are bunted on the ground. Allowing the bat to dip causes pop-ups and foul tips.

Be sure the barrel of the bat extends across home plate to ensure full plate coverage. To check, practice squaring around and then let go of the bat. If the bat drops over all of home plate, you're achieving full plate coverage. If a section of the plate is not covered (usually the outside portion of the plate), make the proper adjustment to your stance position.

RAISE THE BARREL

While waiting for the pitch, raise the barrel end of the bat slightly. Do not hold the bat parallel to the ground. Why? As the pitch is en route to home plate, you'll naturally allow the barrel to slightly dip. This is a recipe for a pop-up or foul tip. Your goal is to bunt the ball on the ground. Start with the barrel raised so it's parallel (or just above parallel) at contact.

When bunting the ball, pretend you're catching the ball with the bat. There should be some "give" with the bat upon contact. This produces a soft hit. A ball bunted too hard will reach infielders quickly and may give them time to force out the lead runner. Accept the ball with your hands and give. Do not push the barrel out to meet the ball. A little touch will go a long way when sacrifice bunting.

See the ball on the ground before running to first base. A common mistake hitters make is that they start moving toward first prematurely. If you're moving toward first before contact, tracking the ball becomes difficult. Your mechanics break down and you'll risk popping the ball up, fouling it off, bunting it too hard, or missing the ball completely. See the ball on the ground and then break out of the batter's box.

WHEN DO I SQUARE AROUND OR PIVOT?

Because you're sacrifice bunting, you're not trying to deceive the defense. Give yourself enough time to get into the proper position. As soon as the pitcher rocks back, square around or pivot. This allows you enough time to set up correctly and execute. If the pitcher employs a rapid motion, set up to bunt a little sooner. Remember, this is a sacrifice bunt. Do whatever it takes to bunt the ball effectively.

WHERE DO I BUNT THE BALL?

The direction of the bunt depends on the game situation. With a runner on first base, the general rule is to force the first baseman to field the ball. When a runner is on second base and you're advancing her to third, bunt the ball to third base. The third baseman will have a difficult time fielding the ball and turning to throw to third to get the runner. Most likely, she'll only have time to get the out at first base.

These are general rules, but changing defensive strategies may dictate where you want to bunt the ball. The first or third baseman may stay at their position and rely on the pitcher to cover that region. If this is the case, bunt the ball to the side the pitcher is covering. Pitching the ball and then quickly getting into position to field a bunt is not an easy task for a pitcher to execute. The second baseman creeps in at times as well, so it is advantageous for you to understand game situations.

Directing the ball is dictated by the angle of the bat. If you wish to bunt the ball to the third base side and you're a right-handed hitter, pull the handle back (in toward your body) and push the barrel forward. The ball will be deflected towards third base. To bunt to first, do the opposite. Push the handle forward and pull the handle back. The angle of the bat is what directs the ball.

COMMON BUNTING MISTAKES

1. *Letting the barrel dip below parallel.* This produces foul tips, pop-ups, and missed pitches.
2. *Failing to hold the bat out in front of you.* Holding the bat too far in toward your body makes it difficult to see the pitch hit the bat. Extend your arms and then allow some flexion. This improves your hand-to-eye coordination.
3. *Running to first before bunting the ball.* Sacrifice bunting means you're sacrificing your at bat. Remain stationary and see the ball hit the ground. Running too early produces inaccurate and inconsistent results.
4. *Failing to bend at the knees.* You must bend your legs when bunting. It puts you in a more athletic position. It also allows you to lower your body to bunt low strikes, rather than dropping the bat down to the ball.
5. *Failure to achieve full plate coverage.* By not moving closer to the plate before squaring to bunt, the outside portion of the plate is left unprotected. Pitchers can spot this weakness and exploit it.

Drag Bunting

Drag bunting is when you bunt the softball in hopes of earning a base hit. To accomplish this, you must bunt the ball into an open area, while building some momentum toward first base. Fast runners often use drag bunting as a means to reach first base safely.

A drag bunt is to the pull-side of the field. Right-handed hitters drag bunt toward the third baseline and left-handed hitters to the first baseline. Because a pitcher stands at close range between both foul lines, it's important to bunt the ball as close to the foul line as possible. If the ball is bunted toward the pitcher, she can easily field the ball and record the out at first base. A general rule among bunters is "if you miss, miss foul." Do not miss to the middle of the infield.

LEFT-HANDED DRAG

Left-handed hitters are more likely to drag bunt because they are a step or two closer to first base from the left-handed batter's box. To do so, stand near the back of the batter's box in your regular stance. As the pitcher starts her wind-up, step toward the pitcher with your rear foot using a crossover step. Slide your top hand up the bat as you move toward the pitch. Angle the bat so the end cap of the bat points toward the shortstop. Keep the barrel of the bat angled upward to make sure the ball is bunted on the ground. As the pitch enters the hitting zone, cradle the bat around the outside of the ball so you pull it with you. As the ball is bunted, continue running toward first base.

All of this is executed on the move. Timing is of the essence. You must time the pitcher's wind-up and the speed of her pitches before stepping up to the plate. If you start your crossover step too soon or too late, you will have difficulty executing.

When bunting the ball to the first-base side, check the positioning of the defenders. If the second baseman is playing up, bunt the ball as close to the first baseline as possible. If the first baseman is playing up and hugging the line, bunt the ball toward the second-base position. When drag bunting, hit the ball hard enough to get it past the pitcher's mound.

RIGHT-HANDED DRAG

A drag bunt for a right-handed hitter is a little different. If you're right-handed, wait until the moment just before the pitcher releases the ball. At this time, drop your right foot back and align it with the first basepath. Slide your top hand up the barrel of the bat and push it out in front of home plate so the end cap points to

Cross over with your rear foot and extend the bat out over home plate. Use your top hand to keep the barrel raised, which helps bunt the ball on the ground.

Drop your rear foot back and push the bat out in front of home plate. Angle the bat (pushing the barrel out) so it deflects the ball toward the third baseline.

the second-base position. Keep the barrel raised to make sure you bunt the ball on the ground.

Again, this must be executed while moving toward first base. Timing is critical in rendering positive results. The third baseman is nearly always playing in, so bunt the ball as close to the third baseline as possible. If the third baseman is playing extremely close, consider bunting the ball to the shortstop position. You must bunt the ball harder to make sure it gets past the pitcher.

A GOOD TIME FOR A DRAG BUNT

- Leading off an inning.
- Late innings of a close game when you need a base runner.
- Your team is being dominated by a tough pitcher.
- You're struggling at the plate and need something to get you going.

Suicide Squeeze

When your team needs a run late in the game, the suicide squeeze is a great weapon to pull from your arsenal. If executed correctly, the suicide squeeze is nearly impossible to defend. Its name stems from what transpires during a failed mission—suicide for the runner. Practice the suicide squeeze regularly to make sure you don't put one of your teammates in a precarious position.

What is a suicide squeeze? It occurs with a runner on third base and less than two outs. Both the hitter and base runner must be aware that the squeeze play is on. The hitter stands in the batter's box in her normal stance. As the pitcher plants her stride foot (just before releasing the ball), the hitter quickly squares around to bunt. The runner breaks for home plate as the ball is released. The hitter bunts the ball fairly as the runner sprints for home, never breaking stride. The defense is basically defenseless. They will not have enough time to field the ball, throw to home plate, and tag the runner out.

As the hitter, you must be aware of several key points to carry out your assignment. Do not square too soon. If you slow bunt, the pitcher can alter the location of her pitch and make it impossible for you to make contact with the ball. If that happens, the runner is a dead duck.

Bunt the ball on the ground. A bunt in the air could result in a double play, a disastrous result to a creative play. Last but not least, you must bunt the ball no matter where it is pitched. You are not looking for a strike, simply the ball. Do whatever it takes to get your bat on the ball. You must protect the runner or she will be an easy out.

Bunt-and-Run

The bunt-and-run play is implemented to advance a base runner two bases with a sacrifice bunt. This play is most commonly used with a runner on first base and one out.

As the pitch is released, the runner takes off for second base. The hitter squares around and bunts the ball to third base. The base runner never stops running. She rounds second and looks to continue to third base. Because the third baseman is fielding the ball and throwing to first and the shortstop is breaking toward second base on the steal, third base may be left open. If the catcher covers third, it becomes a foot race to the bag. When properly executed, the runner should be able to reach third base safely, sometimes without even a throw.

It's very important for the hitter to force the third baseman to field the ball. Make her move forward to field the ball, making it extremely difficult for her to get back to third base before the base runner arrives.

Consider trying this with a runner on second base. It is very risky, and because of that, is rarely attempted. This play can work, however, if the runner on second is very fast and you catch the defense sleeping.

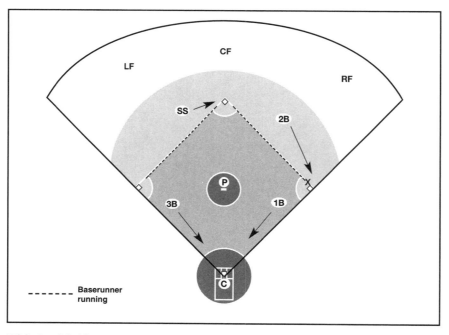

With the third baseman charging and the shortstop covering second base, third base is left open. If the catcher is not covering, the base runners should round second base and continue running to third base.

The runner takes off for third on the pitch and the batter bunts the ball down the first baseline. The runner never breaks stride and continues to home plate on the throw to first. Upon fielding the ball, the first baseman turns her back to throw to first base. She'll never see the runner streaking home. If you're successful at pulling this off, it's a great way to steal a run.

Hit-and-Run

The hit-and-run play is commonly used to spark a struggling offense. Whether the team is having trouble scoring runs or a hitter is hesitant to pull the trigger at the plate, a hit-and-run can turn the key to the engine's ignition system.

A hit-and-run can occur with a runner on first base or first and second base. The runner (or runners) steals on the pitch. The hitter swings the bat regardless of the pitch's location. Her job is to hit the ball (put it in play) to protect the runner.

The runner breaking accomplishes two things. First, it opens a hole in the infield. Either the second baseman or shortstop will begin moving to cover second base on the steal. Their position in the

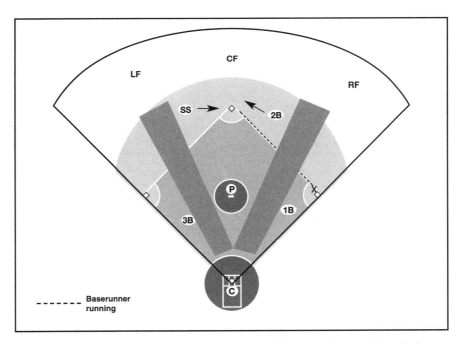

With the middle infielders shifting toward second base on the steal, the hitting lanes widen for the batter.

field is left vacant, leaving a larger-than-usual hole on one side of the infield. Secondly, putting the base runner in motion protects the offense from grounding into a double play. If the batter hits a ground ball that is fielded cleanly, the force at second base is taken out of the equation because the runner broke on the pitch. She'll easily beat the throw.

Keep the barrel above the ball on the hit and run play. Hitting the ball on the ground allows the runner to advance and may also earn you a base hit.

The best-case scenario on this play is that the batter hits a ground ball through a hole in the infield and the runner races from first all the way to third base. (If there are runners on first and second base, a run scores.)

For this play to work, the batter must be capable of making consistent contact. Should she swing through the pitch, the runner is in danger of being thrown out on the steal.

Assuming you're the hitter, choke up an inch on the bat, and shorten your swing. You're not trying to hit the ball with maximum power. Contact is the primary goal and hitting the ball on the ground is the secondary goal. To accomplish both, see the ball as long as possible before committing your hands to a swing. This keeps you from getting fooled on the pitch. Also, try to hit the top of the ball. Keep your hands (and barrel) above the ball to increase your chances of hitting the ball on the ground.

If you're good enough to hit the ball on the ground and direct it through the hole left vacant in the infield, than you're a perfect candidate for more hit-and-run plays. When executed properly, the hit-and-run play is indefensible, and to fans of the game, a work of art.

Moving the Runner from Second Base

When a runner advances to second base with no outs, coaches often give the bunt sign to the batter. A successful sacrifice bunt moves the runner to third base with one out. A fly ball to the outfield now scores the runner.

Another option is to allow the batter to move the runner with a swing. A ground ball to the right side of second base allows the runner to safely advance to third base. The good part is that there is a chance that the batter may hit the ball in the hole for a base hit instead of sacrificing an out.

Perfecting this craft is entirely different for right- and left-handed hitters. The right-handed hitter must hit the ball to the opposite field, while left-handed hitters must pull the ball.

If you're a right-handed hitter, look for a pitch in the middle or outside part of the strike zone. Let the ball travel deep into the hitting zone. In other words, let the ball get close to you. Your swing should be later rather than sooner. Allow the barrel of the bat to trail your hands, so it's angled toward the right side of the infield. (Remember, this is a situational swing, not your customary swing.) Minimize your hip rotation and keep the barrel of the bat above the ball to ensure hitting the ball on the ground.

If you're left-handed, pull the ball. Look for a pitch in the middle or inside part of the strike zone. Start your swing early so you make contact out in front of home plate. Your top hand should roll early, so the bat is angled to the right side of second base. Rotate your hips fully and keep the barrel on top of the ball to manufacture a ground ball.

SLAP HITTING

A slap hit is essentially a drag bunt from the left side of the plate where a hitter takes an abbreviated swing at the ball. Similar to drag bunting, slap hitters start from the rear end of the box, take a few steps forward, and strike the ball as they're in motion. This gives them momentum as they run to first base.

Slap hitting is generally taught to players who boast exceptional running speed. It's practiced only from the left-hand side of the batter's box. Left-handers may acquire this skill with greater ease, but it's also employed by fleet-footed, right-handed hitters who are able to make the transition to the left-hand side of the box. By mastering the skill of slap hitting, you can become a multidimensional hitter.

To master this skill, first understand that the ball has to be hit on the ground. Anything hit in the air is almost certain to be an out. Most slap hitters like to hit the ball toward the shortstop. The shortstop position is deeper than the third or first baseman and has a longer throw than the second baseman. Consequently, the shortstop position is the easiest area for a hitter to beat out an infield ground ball. Superior slap hitters vary the spots they hit to depending on the positioning of the fielders. These players possess phenomenal bat control and wreak havoc on defenses.

Choke and Poke

To properly execute the slap hit, start near the back of the batter's box. Choke up on the bat an inch or two. This makes the bat lighter and easier to control. As the pitcher nears her release point, take a short step forward with your lead foot. Next, take a crossover step with your rear foot. This step is to be taken as the pitch is released. Keep your hands held back and shoulders square to the pitcher. Although your body is moving forward and leaning toward the first baseline, your head and shoulders must remain square to the ball. You've got to see it to hit it.

Stay Square to the Ball

Keeping the shoulders square also keeps the hands and bat back. If you carry the hands forward, the bat will drag and you'll pop the ball up. As the pitch enters the hitting zone, strike downward at the ball in a short, cutting motion. Keep your eyes down on the point of contact and barrel above the ball. Use an abbreviated follow-through and take off for first base.

As mentioned, keeping the hands back is very important to hitting the ball on the ground, but it also serves another purpose. It allows you to stop your swing and take the pitch should it be out of the strike zone. Carrying the hands forward leads to poor swings at unfavorable pitches.

To develop your slap-hitting skills, start off on a tee. Learn the swing first, and then add the feet. The slap swing is different from your natural swing, so you've got to retrain your hands and wrists. Once you've become comfortable with the swing, begin to walk up to the tee and slap the ball. Move on to short tosses, and finally, take live batting practice. Timing is critical in slap hitting, so countless swings are crucial to developing rhythm. Keep in mind that the timing will be slightly different with every pitcher you face. The speed of their delivery and velocity of pitches factors into

When setting up to slap hit, take your stance at the rear of the batter's box.

Cross over with your rear foot to start your momentum toward first base. Allow the barrel of the bat to trail your hands (as shown) to hit the ball to the left side of the infield.

when you take that first step forward. Pay attention in the on-deck circle and time the pitcher before you step up to the plate.

Advanced slap hitters are also learning to drive the ball while using the step approach. This makes them more difficult to defend. Infielders will become reluctant to play so close in fear of a ball being driven hard at them. Outfielders will also be hesitant to play extremely shallow.

Right-handed hitters have also begun to develop a slap play to fool defenses and open up hitting lanes. This is sometimes referred to as a "slash play." The batter will slow bunt using the pivot method. As the pitch is about to be released, she pulls the bat back and takes a swing at the pitch (if it's a strike). With the first and third basemen charging, the second baseman moving to cover first and the shortstop moving to cover second, the hitter simply needs to hit the ball on the ground. The defensive players are caught out of position and can only rely on luck to record an out.

GAMES

Situational Batting Practice

During batting practice, designate one round where each of the eight swings has a specific purpose. This is called situational batting practice. Include a round of situational batting practice every day and each player will quickly develop into an adequate situational hitter.

    1st pitch—Sacrifice bunt to first base
    2nd pitch—Sacrifice bunt to third base
    3rd pitch—Squeeze bunt
    4th pitch—Drag bunt
    5th pitch—Hit and run

6th pitch—Advance the runner from second base (ground ball to the right side)

7th pitch—Score the runner from third base (fly ball to the outfield)

8th pitch—Line drive back through the middle

Bunt into the Bucket

Place two five-gallon buckets in fair territory approximately 12 feet away from the nearest point of home plate, one bucket three feet from the third-base line, and one three feet from the first-base line, with the openings facing home plate.

The game is played by giving each player nine sacrifice bunt attempts, divided into three rounds of three bunts each. Each player receives a score based on her bunting proficiency: three points for any ball that rolls into a bucket; two points for any ball bunted that rolls fair between the baseline and the bucket; minus one point for a foul ball, a ball bunted more than four feet into the air, a bunt and miss, or a called strike.

A player may "call her shot" to receive a bonus of five points. To receive the bonus, the player must declare before the pitch into which

Place a bucket along the first baseline and a second bucket along the third baseline. Practice bunting the ball to each side, attempting to direct the ball into the mouth of the bucket.

A "called shot" bunted into the bucket is worth five points.

bucket she will bunt the ball. The player with the most points is declared the winner.

Hit 'Em Where They Ain't

This game is excellent for teaching bat control. When the game situation calls for you to hit a ground ball to the right side of second base, you'll be glad you practiced this game.

The fielders play in a special "shift" defense: against a right-handed hitter, all fielders—except the first baseman—move toward the left side of the field, so that there is only one remaining fielder to the right side of second base. (The first baseman must stay at first base, with her foot in contact with the bag at all times.) Against a left-handed batter, all fielders move to the right side of second base. The remaining players form the offensive team.

Have the pitcher deliver the ball at batting-practice speed. Encourage every hitter to hit the ball to the opposite field. Each player bats until she makes an out. After a hitter makes an out she changes places with one of the fielders. The game continues until every player has batted a minimum of three times.

Next, reverse the game so that the fielders are on the left side of the infield for right-handed hitters and the right side of the infield for left-handed hitters. Look to get the barrel out early in the swing and pull the ball.

Consecutive Hitting Streak

This game is designed to improve your proficiency at executing the hit-and-run play.

The hitter steps up to the plate with the hit-and-run sign activated. A pitcher from your team throws at game speed. The goal of the hitter (who has to swing at every pitch) is to make contact and hit the ball on the ground in fair territory. If she accomplishes this, she stays in the batter's box for another pitch. She continues her streak of successful hits until she misses a pitch, hits a ball in foul territory, or hits the ball in the air. Once the streak is broken, another hitter takes her turn.

The pitcher must vary her pitches and their locations, just as if she were pitching in a game. Keep count and see who totals the most consecutive hits.

Before the pitcher releases the ball, know where you're going with the ball if it's hit to you. Then, playing defense just becomes a matter of execution.

8

DEFENSIVE STRATEGY

How many sports can you think of where the defense starts with the ball? Take baseball out of the equation because it's a sport so similar to softball. Besides baseball and softball, how many other sports are there? You can't think of any, can you? Fast-pitch softball is a unique sport because the defense is the team that starts with the ball. That means that a team's defensive strategy can attempt to dictate play, rather than the defense adjusting to the attacking offense.

There are certain aspects of the game that a defense can never anticipate. Home runs hit over the fence, doubles smashed down the third baseline, seeing-eyed choppers that bounce up the middle, and Texas-league bloopers that drop in the shallow outfield are examples of plays that are indefensible. Your pitcher may be able to do something about it, but once the ball leaves the bat, you've got to react and execute as best as you can.

Other game situations are predictable and can be anticipated. Bunt plays, slap hits, and steals are offensive plays strategically implemented to advance runners and score runs. The defense has the opportunity to set up for and counter these attacks before the ball is put into play.

Bunt Coverages

Pitching dominates fast-pitch softball. Very few runs are scored when teams have adequate pitching. Because of this, a premium is placed on runs—or at a more rudimentary level—base runners. Once a runner reaches base, she becomes a valuable asset to her team and the attention of the offense now focuses on getting her home. Bunt plays are used to advance runners and move them closer to crossing home plate.

Defensive teams should always keep one important thing in mind when fielding a sacrifice bunt—make sure you get an out. The offense is sacrificing an out, so it is essential that you take advantage of that opportunity. Each out secured is another step toward getting back in the dugout and swinging the bats. Use good judgment and make sure you get at least one out on a sacrifice bunt play.

Any time a bunt situation arises, every defensive player must be alert. Each position has a responsibility on the field. The first and third basemen position themselves closer to home plate to field the bunt. The second baseman shifts over to cover first base. The shortstop shifts to cover second or third base, depending on the game situation. The catcher jumps out to field any ball she can get to first. (If another player is able to reach the ball quicker, the catcher must become the field general and call out which base to throw the ball to.) The pitcher is responsible for balls bunted in her area. At times, the third or first baseman may stay closer to her base, leaving the pitcher responsible for fielding shallow balls bunted to either side of the field.

Outfielders must run to a position where they can back up a throw. Left fielders back up all throws to third base, and right fielders back up

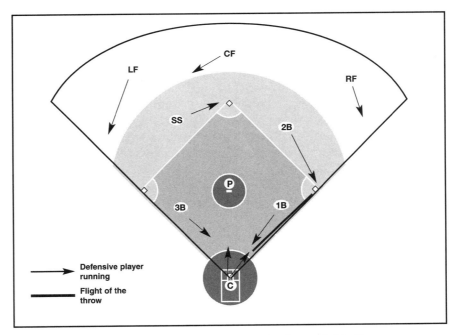

In a bunt situation, with a runner on first base, the first and third baseman charge home plate. The second baseman covers first base and the shortstop covers second base. Outfielders back up bases for possible overthrows.

all throws to first base. Every outfielder is responsible for backing up throws to second base, depending on the angle from which the ball is thrown.

RECOGNIZING WHEN A PLAYER IS BUNTING

- Moves up in the batter's box and closer to home plate.
- Chokes up on the bat.
- Takes a stance that varies in some way from her customary stance.
- Peeks out at the infielders to gauge their positioning.
- Begins to drop her hands as the pitcher begins her delivery.
- Begins to pivot or shift her feet as the pitcher begins her delivery.

RUNNER ON FIRST BASE

With a runner on first base, there are two possibilities: throw the ball to second base to force out the lead runner, or throw the ball to first base and get an out. Obviously, forcing out the lead runner presents the most attractive outcome. A well-placed bunt, however, eliminates any chance of getting the lead runner. Get the sure out at first base.

The cornermen (first and third basemen) move up until they're about 30 feet from home plate (approximately halfway between the base and home plate). As soon as the batter signals that she's bunting, charge home plate. Upon fielding the ball, listen to what your catcher is calling out. If she yells, "First!" or "One!" square your feet to first base and throw to the base. If she calls "Second!" or "Two!" square your feet to second base and throw to the base. By the location and speed of the bunt, anticipate which base your catcher will tell you to throw the ball.

With the cornermen charging, the second baseman covers first base and the shortstop covers second base. This leaves third base open. Base runners advancing to second on this play often continue running to reach

A choked bat or crossover step is a clear indication that a player is bunting.

third base, hoping no one will be covering the bag. If the third baseman fields the ball, the catcher is responsible for covering third base.

RUNNER ON SECOND BASE

With a runner on second base, look to get an out at first base. There is no force play at third base, so the chances of throwing out the lead runner are slim. To catch the lead runner, the shortstop has to cover third base. This is a difficult play and should only be attempted if the base runner is slow. In most cases, make sure of an out and throw to first base.

With runners on first and second base, there is a chance of getting the lead runner because there's a force play at third. To get the out at third, the shortstop has to leave her position before the pitch and cover third base. This enables the third baseman to charge in and field balls along the third baseline. The shortstop slides behind her, and covers third base for the possible force play. The ball has to be bunted hard and directly at a fielder to have enough time to force out the runner advancing to third base.

This coverage, called a "rotation coverage," is an advanced bunt coverage and should only be used in desperate situations. One other hole in this coverage is that second base is left open. There is no

With the first baseman playing in for the bunt, the second baseman is responsible for covering the first base bag on a bunt play.

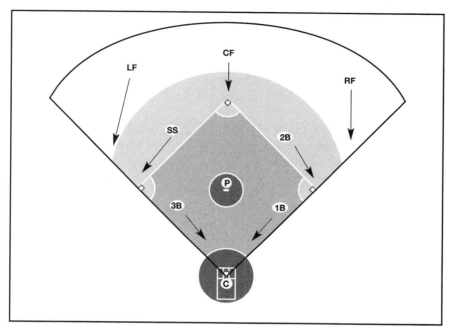

With runners on first and second, the shortstop covers third base and the center fielder runs in to cover second base.

chance of getting the runner at second, reducing the chances of turning a double play.

The Suicide Squeeze

The suicide squeeze is a bunt play where a runner from third breaks for home plate as the ball is released. The batter squares around (later than normal) and bunts the ball. The batter must make contact with the ball to protect the runner, so she'll bunt pitches that are even out of the strike zone. When properly executed, the suicide squeeze play is nearly impossible to defend.

The first chance of defending this play lies with the pitcher. If she notices something out of the ordinary from the batter, she can call for a pitch-out. A pitch-out is a pitch thrown way outside so that the batter has no chance of reaching the ball. The catcher must conspire with the pitcher on this pitch call. As the ball is being released, she rises out of her crouch and steps to the side of the unattended batter's box. It's used in defense of suicide squeeze plays and steals.

Something that appears out of the ordinary might be how the batter takes her stance, her positioning in the batter's box (moving forward and standing closer to the plate), or a peculiar confirmation signal she might relay to the third-base coach. The pitcher might even pick up on the sudden, undivided attention from the opposing dugout. Under any of these circumstances, call for a pitch-out so the batter is unable to reach the ball. The runner breaking from third will be a dead duck, caught running toward home plate while the catcher holds the ball.

If the bunt is properly executed, the only chance is to field the ball and shovel-toss it to the catcher in one motion. Use your momentum as you run up to the ball to fuel your toss to the catch. Advanced players never let the ball enter the glove's pocket. They use the outside of their glove and hand to field the ball and release it as quickly as possible. Even in using this technique, the ball may not get home in time. The ball would have to be bunted hard and directly at an infielder. In most cases, concede the run and get the out at first base.

SAFETY SQUEEZE

The other type of bunt play used to score a run is called the safety squeeze. On this play, the runner at third shuffles off the base upon the pitcher's release, waits to see that the ball is bunted on the ground, and then breaks for home. This play is not as risky for the offense, but also affords the defense more time to make the play. The runner won't get home as quickly and can be thrown out on the play. It entails perfect execution, but is possible.

Again, the ball has to be bunted hard and at an infielder to give you a chance. Charge the plate as soon as you see the batter show bunt. If the ball is bunted to you, field the ball on the run and underhand toss it to the catcher. Keep your toss low and to the third-base side of home plate. Any ball that takes you to your right or left will have to be fielded and thrown to first base.

First and Third Double Steal

Base runners can be used as decoys by the offense. With runners on first and third base, a double steal is commonly used to score a run. (This play is especially popular with two outs.) The base runner from first breaks for second base as the pitch is released. In essence, she's used as the decoy to divert attention and draw a throw from the catcher. Once the catcher releases the ball, the runner from third base breaks for home. To thwart this offensive scheme, the defense must execute a counterattack.

FAKE THROW TO SECOND

A simple plan is to fake a throw to second base. Concede second base to the base runner in the hopes of catching the runner at third base

To sell the fake throw to second base, the catcher has to display her natural throwing motion right up until the point of release.

breaking prematurely. If she scampers too far off the base, pick her off with a throw to third, or catch her in a rundown. Run straight at her and force her back to third base. Once she commits to running back to third, deliver the ball to your third baseman to tag the runner out.

In order to pull this play off, the catcher has to convince the runner at third that she's actually throwing the ball to second base. The catcher must pop out of her catcher's stance upon receiving the pitch, shift her feet, and align them for a throw to second, step and create realistic arm action. Everything should look the same as if you were throwing until it comes to releasing the ball. At that time, simply hold onto the ball, follow through, and then quickly look down to third base. If the catcher's actions are convincing, the runner will take the bait and begin her sprint toward home plate.

MIDDLE INFIELDER INTERCEPTS THE THROW

A second counterattack is to have a middle infielder step in front of second base, intercept the throw from the catcher, and then rifle a strike home to catch the runner stealing from third base. Which infielder, the second baseman or shortstop, intercepts the throw depends on which player is covering second base on the steal. If the second baseman covers the bag, the shortstop moves in front of the base to take the throw.

Most offensive coaches tell the base runner at third not to break until she sees the ball take flight from the catcher. Your plan is to fool the runner into thinking the ball is going all the way to second base. But if the middle infielder steps forward and fields an accurate throw, she should have enough time to throw out the streaking runner from third base.

PITCHER CUT-OFF

A third defensive strategy calls for the pitcher to cut off the throw to second base. After she delivers the ball home, the pitcher remains standing in front of the rubber. The catcher jumps up and fires the ball in the direction of second base. (The catcher's goal is to throw the ball straight back at the head of the pitcher. If the ball is thrown lower, it will be obvious that the throw is intended for the pitcher.) The pitcher sticks her glove up and snares the ball in midflight. She then turns to third base and attempts to pick off the runner at third.

CALLING THE PLAY

To execute an efficient defense of the first and third double steal, each player on the field must be cognizant of the defensive scheme. A player on the field must give a signal to her teammates so they all know their responsibilities.

Play-calls are given by the coach from the dugout. The coach may elect the catcher or third baseman to relay the signal on the field. Whether the signs come from the catcher or third base, each player must divert their attention to the player flashing the signals. This includes the outfielders, who will be backing up the play.

Review all defensive signals with a teammate before each game. It's your responsibility as a team member to be aware of each play and its sign. Don't let your teammates down by failing to recognize the signs.

Rundowns

Nothing stings a defense more than catching a player in a rundown and failing to register an out. Rundowns occur when a base runner is caught between two bases. The goal of the defense is to tag the runner out quickly, using the fewest number of throws.

The key to executing rundowns is making the runner commit. Force her to commit to a base by running hard at her. Running hard at your opponent results in one of three scenarios. 1) You'll catch up to her and be able to tag her out yourself. 2) She'll stall her run in an attempt to draw a throw and then retreat back to the opposite base. In this case, you'll also be able to tag her out yourself. 3) She'll continue running all the way to a base, with which you'll toss the ball to your teammate covering the bag to tag her out.

Whenever possible, run your opponent back to her original base. For example, if the runner is caught between second and third base, run her back to second base. That way, if something breaks down and you fail to tag her out, she still hasn't advanced to the next base.

When you're holding the ball in a rundown, run hard at the runner with the ball held up by your ear. This keeps the ball visible to your teammate covering the base, and also allows you to pump fake. If the runner is looking back at you as she runs, a pump fake (fake throw) can fool her into to stopping and changing direction. Continue running and tag her out.

If you're covering a base and awaiting a throw, give your team-mate a clear throwing lane. Don't stand in line with the runner. Once the runner gets close enough to the base (about 10–12 feet), call out "Ball!" This tells your teammate to deliver the ball. If the opponent continues running to the base, catch the ball and apply a tag. If she stops, catch the ball with your momentum moving forward and tag her out.

Pick-Offs

Aggressive base runners can wreak havoc on defenses. Not only are they capable of advancing bases amidst the slightest opportunities, but they also warrant additional attention from the pitcher, catcher, and infielders. This takes focus away from another dangerous player—the batter.

Courageous base runners are also susceptible. They're risk-takers and can be stricken from the base paths if the defense becomes offensive-minded. Pick-off plays can turn a worrisome situation into a free out.

FIRST BASE PICK-OFFS

The pick-off to first base is the easiest to execute. As the pitch is released, the base runner bolts forward and shuffles from the base in anticipation of a batted ball or passed ball. Aggressive base runners tend to have their momentum moving forward as the ball crosses home plate, rewarding them with an excellent jump if the ball is hit. When the ball is not hit or taken, the runner is stranded far from the base, with the weight of her body shifted onto her front foot. This is an opportunity to exploit.

A pick-off throw can accomplish one of two things. It can place an "out" on the scoreboard, or, at the very least, tame the base runner's lead.

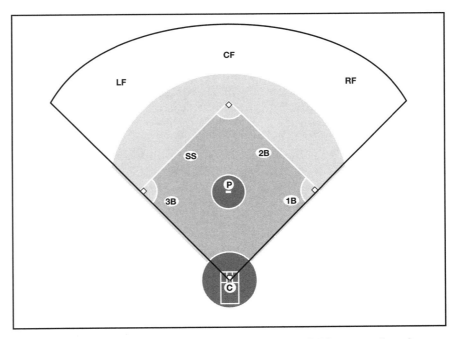

When your team must stop the run from scoring, the infielders move in to keep the runner at third base.

With a right-handed batter at the plate, call for a pitch-out. As the ball is released, the first baseman creeps back toward the bag. As the ball travels toward home plate, the catcher shuffles over to the outside part of the plate, catches the ball, and immediately fires the ball to the first base. If the runner at first is not paying attention, she'll have little chance getting back to the base in time.

When holding a comfortable lead late in the game, always get the sure out at first base.

Another option in this play is to have the second baseman sneak behind the runner and cover first base. That way, the runner will perceive no danger, because the first baseman remains in her sight in front of her. The second baseman must slip behind the runner as the pitch is delivered to reach first base in time for the throw.

Advanced catchers bearing strong arms don't need to call for a pitch-out. Simply set up on the outside of the plate. As you receive the ball, drop to your knees and throw to first base. It's a quicker delivery, and a throw that is impossible to detect by the base runner.

SECOND BASE AND THIRD BASE PICK-OFFS

Second base pick-offs require longer throws, but can also be effective. Players take longer leads off second base, which allows more time for the throw to arrive. Upon the signal of the second baseman or shortstop, the catcher receives the pitch and makes an immediate throw to second base. Regardless of which player is covering, throw the ball directly to second base.

With a runner on third base, consider a pick-off attempt with a left-handed batter at the plate. This provides you with a clear throwing lane with no obstructions. The third baseman sets up to the third base-side of the bag after the pitch is delivered. Stand up and rifle a strike to the infield-side of the bag. This play is risky, because an errant throw results in a run scored for the opposition. Make sure you've got a legitimate chance at catching the runner and make a strong, accurate throw.

RUNNER ON THIRD—MIDDLE INFIELD DEPTH

With a runner on third base and less than two outs, the middle infield must determine the depth at which they'll defend the field. Should they play deep to increase their range on a batted ball and concede the run? Should they move up halfway and even with the base to create the option of throwing to home plate or first base? Should they move in and go for the runner at the plate?

These decisions are based on the game situation. In a game that is close, you're not at liberty to be soft on defense and should play halfway or all the way in. Playing halfway can inhibit the runner from breaking for home on contact. If the runner holds, you can look her back and throw to first. If she breaks immediately, throw her out at the plate.

By playing all the way in, the runner is taking a huge risk by breaking on contact. The ball gets to the infielders quickly, giving them time to field the ball and make an accurate throw in time to get the runner.

Why not play in all the time in these situations? Playing so close to the batter decreases your range dramatically. Balls hit more than a step or two to your right or left will glance past you and into the outfield. The amount of territory you're able to defend is minimal.

If you're winning by a comfortable margin, play back, and get the out. When you have a big lead, outs are more important than allowing the opposition to narrow the margin by one run.

GAMES

Pickle

This game requires three or more players and two bases. If you don't have bases, use hats, sweatshirts, or extra gloves as bases. A defensive player is stationed at each base, one of whom holds a softball. The offensive player (or base runner) starts in the middle of the two bases. On the call of "pickle," the defensive team attempts to tag out the base runner. The base runner runs back and forth, avoiding being tagged out while attempting to reach a base safely.

The runner earns one point for each throw made by the defensive players. The more time she's able to stay alive, the greater amount of throws she'll accumulate. If the runner reaches a base safely, she earns three bonus points.

Continue playing until each contestant runs in a pickle at least three times. Add up all of the points earned and the player with the most points wins.

This game is designed to practice rundowns. Defensive players work on tagging the runner out using the fewest throws possible. Base runners also practice how to avoid being tagged out in a rundown situation.

Situation Softball

Set up a defensive team in the field. The defense should include players at all positions including the pitcher and catcher. A team of five players stands at home plate and represents the offensive squad. A coach is alongside the players at home plate with a fungo bat and softball.

The coach tosses the ball up and bats it into play. The runner takes off from home plate as if she's hit the ball. Once the ball is in play, the defense and runner treat it as an ordinary game. If runners are safe, they stay on base and react to the next hit. Once the defensive team records three outs, the bases are cleared. The offensive team remains at bat for three consecutive innings, and tries to score as many runs as possible.

After three innings, the five players take the position of five defensive players and those players become the new offensive team. The team of five that scores the most runs wins the game.

Situation softball presents the defensive team with all types of game scenarios. The coach controls each hit and can concoct a variety of game-action circumstances that are difficult to simulate in ordinary practice drills.

DRILLS
First and Third Fire Drill

With your defensive team in the field, place runners on first and third base. As the pitcher delivers a pitch home, the runner on first breaks for second base. The catcher makes a throw toward second base, which is intercepted by the shortstop or second baseman (alternate with each throw). The runner from third breaks on the throw in an attempt to steal home. The infielder then throws home to cut down the runner.

The runner stealing second base is to continue running to third base. After applying the tag to the runner at home, the catcher throws the ball to third base. The base runner then stops midway between second and third base, getting into a rundown. The defense attempts to complete a double play by tagging the runner out between second and third base.

If executed correctly, the defense can record two outs on the play. If not, it's conceivable that the defense records no outs, and a run scores. The First and Third Fire Drill is an excellent exercise that forces every player on defense to be alert.

Ricochet Rabbit

This drill is a favorite of catchers. It involves pick-off throws to a variety of bases at any given time.

With your infield at their positions, place runners at first, second, and third base. For the sake of the drill, runners are told to take very aggressive leads on each pitch. As each pitch is delivered, position players will sneak around to cover their base to get into position for a pick-off throw. Who is the target of the pick-off is at the discretion of the catcher.

After each pitch, the catcher will fire a pick-off throw to the base of her choice. In addition to improving the defense's execution on pick-offs, base runners will develop a sense of how far is too far when taking a lead.

9

CONDITIONING

A stronger, well-conditioned athlete is a better athlete. Case closed. Do you want to run faster, throw harder, hit the ball with more power, and play defense with increased range? If the answer is yes, it's time to start a conditioning program.

Gone are the myths that hitters, pitchers, and defensive players suffer diminished skills by strengthening their bodies. The stereotype that women are in uncharted waters when entering the weight room has also passed. Girls of all ages condition their bodies to enhance performance and reduce the risk of injury. Take advantage of the opportunity to improve your body and your game. Strength and fitness yield not only physical benefits but give you a psychological edge as well.

To achieve maximum results as a softball player, you've got to train hard. This includes weight training, cardiovascular training, flexibility training, and agility training. Each type of training is necessary to become a complete player. Weight training increases bat speed and power, improves arm strength, and elevates your speed on the base paths. Flexibility training keeps you loose and limber. This enables you to stay fluid and rhythmic while the body is in motion. Cardiovascular training keeps your legs strong throughout an entire game. When the game is on the line in the late innings, healthy legs allow you to maintain a solid base for balance and power. Endurance training can also help you leg that double into a triple. Finally, there is agility training. It works on your balance and improves quickness. Softball is a game of quick, explosive movements and agility training allows you to execute those movements swiftly and from a balanced position.

There is more to becoming a complete softball player than simply fielding, throwing, and hitting riseballs. Players must condition their bodies to maximize their ability.

FLEXIBILITY TRAINING

It's sensible to introduce conditioning with flexibility training. Anytime you engage in physical activity, start with stretching exercises. Prior to practices, games or personal workouts, always stretch to perform effectively and avoid injury.

Before stretching, jog lightly for two to four minutes. This loosens your joints and muscles and acts as your body's wake-up call. Once you've finished jogging, begin stretching. Ideally, you want to hold each stretch for a few seconds until you feel the muscles relax. Then increase the stretch until you feel resistance again.

These stretching exercises start from the ankles and move upward. Refer to this routine each time you workout, practice, or play a game.

Ankle Stretch

Lift your foot off the ground and balance on one leg. Point your toe toward the ground and make circles with your foot to loosen the ankle joint. Make 10 circles and then switch feet. After completing two sets of 10, make counter-clockwise circles with your feet 10 times.

Calf and Achilles Tendon Stretch

Lean against a post, the dugout wall, or a fence with your hands pressed firmly against the object you're leaning on. Move one leg 6 to eight inches backward, keeping both feet flat on the ground. Bend the front knee forward and allow the heel of the rear foot to raise off the ground. Keep the toe of your rear foot on the ground. Hold the stretch for 10 seconds and then switch legs. Continue until you complete three sets of stretches for each leg.

Upper Hamstring Stretch

To stretch the upper hamstring muscle, lie flat on your back and pull your knee into your chest. Hold the stretch with both hands and keep your opposite leg on the ground

Lay flat on your back. Bend your left leg at the knee and raise it toward your midsection. Grab the shin of your left leg with both hands and pull into your midsection. Pull it up toward your chin as far as possible. Your right leg and back should remain as flat as possible on the ground. Hold the stretch for 10 seconds and then switch legs. Complete three sets for each leg.

Lower Hamstring Stretch

Standing erect with your feet close together, cross your right foot over your left foot and bend at the waist. Grab your ankles or feet (whatever your flexibility allows) with both hands. Hold the stretch for 10 seconds and switch. Try to increase your stretch with each set.

Quadricep Stretch

Standing erect, bend your right leg at the knee so your right foot raises behind you. Reach

To stretch the lower hamstring, cross one foot over the other, bend at the waist, and reach for the ground. Grab your ankles, feet, or touch your palms to the ground.

Grab the instep of your foot with your same-side hand. Pull up so your heel touches your rear end. This stretch loosens the quadricep muscle.

Sit down, bend one leg at the knee, and cross it over the other leg (as shown). Apply pressure to your knee with your opposite-side arm, pushing down as you twist your midsection.

down with your right hand and grab the instep of your right foot. Pull your foot up to your buttocks, while maintaining your balance on your left leg. Hold the stretch for ten seconds and then relax and switch legs.

Torso Stretch

Sit on the ground with your legs stretched outward in front of you. Bend your right leg at the knee, slide your right foot inward toward your buttocks, and grab your right knee with both hands. Next, lift your right foot over your left leg and place it on the outside of your left knee. Put your right hand on the ground by your right side (for balance) and place your left on the outside of your right knee. Pull the knee to the left to feel a stretch in the right portion of your torso. Hold for 10 seconds and switch.

Lower Back

Lie flat on your stomach on the ground. Use both hands to push your upper body up off the ground, but keep your entire lower body (from the waist down) pressed against the ground. Hold this position for 10 seconds and then rest. Repeat this four or five times to stretch the lower back.

Upper Back Stretch

Holding your hands out in front of you, lock them together with your fingers. Raise your hands above your head and stretch your arms up toward the sky. Turn your hands over so your palms face the sky. Hold your arms up in this extended position for 15 seconds. Rest and repeat five times.

Shoulder Stretch

Lay your right arm across your chest. Grab your right elbow with your left hand and pull your right arm up and to the left. Hold the stretch for 10 seconds and then relax. Repeat the same exercise, this time pulling your left arm across your body. Stretch each arm for three sets.

Neck Stretch

Relax your neck and drop your head downward. Slowly roll your head in a clockwise motion around and around five times. Take a rest (so you don't get too dizzy) and then slowly roll it around in a counter-clockwise motion. Repeat each direction three times.

Tricep

Lift your right arm directly back over your right shoulder. Reach over your head with your left hand, grab your right elbow, and pull it back. Pull it back as far as it can go without experiencing pain. Hold the stretch for 10 seconds and switch arms. Stretch each tricep for three sets.

Grab your elbow with your opposite hand and pull it across your chest. This stretch loosens the exterior shoulder muscles.

This exercise stretches the tricep and shoulder muscle regions. Raise your arm behind your head and over your shoulder. Grab your elbow with your opposite arm and pull back until you feel a stretch.

Extend your arm outward so your palm faces the sky. Grab your fingers and pull down to stretch your wrist and forearm.

Forearms

Extend your right arm out in front of you and turn your hand over so your palm faces the sky. Grab the right-hand fingers with your left hand and pull them down. Keep the right arm extended as you do this. Hold the stretch for 10 seconds and then switch arms. Next, allow the palm to face down and pull up on the fingers. Hold this stretch for 10 seconds and then switch. Repeat each stretch three times.

CARDIOVASCULAR TRAINING

Cardiovascular training is also referred to as endurance training. It builds stamina in your muscular and respiratory systems. It keeps your heart rate under control during competition, which allows you to play relaxed on an even keel. Pitching, hitting, fielding, baserunning, and throwing are difficult skills to master when you're out of breath gasping for air. Cardiovascular training also conditions your body to play an entire game without feeling fatigued.

Local fitness centers provide a variety of ways to build endurance. Aerobic classes, step class, spinning, biking, and kickboxing classes are all enjoyable methods of achieving your goals. Fitness machines such as the Stairmaster and treadmills also offer excellent opportunities for cardiovascular workouts. If you have access to a local gym, it will be a great resource for you to fulfill your fitness needs. Joining a gym is highly recommended.

In addition to providing equipment, fitness centers offer trainers who can teach you proper technique. They're educated in devising fitness programs and can create a personal program to satisfy your individual needs. You can also pick up new training tips by observing the workouts of other gym members or even connect up with a workout buddy. It's very beneficial to have a workout partner present to push you to work harder, especially on days that you're lacking enthusiasm.

There are plenty of other training methods to fulfill your cardiovascular training needs. Distance running can be performed on back roads, park trails, or outdoor tracks. Bicycling is another activity that builds stamina and leg strength. Sprint intervals improve speed, quickness and explosiveness—all traits that will be of great service to you on the softball field.

Training Can Be Fun

Most young athletes grimace when cardiovascular or endurance training is mentioned, but it doesn't necessarily have to seem like an obligation. Be creative and make it fun. Set up relay races where the losing team has to do sit-ups. Time your runs (both sprints and long distance) and compete with your teammates for the best time.

There are many recreational sports that are enjoyable and are perfect for cardiovascular training. Tennis, indoor soccer, full-court basketball, and racquetball are just a few sports that require running, stopping and starting, and quick recovery. Swimming is another sport that builds strength and endurance.

Playing defense and running the bases may not seem like a lot of running in comparison to sports like basketball, soccer, and lacrosse, but over seven innings, your legs can grow tired. Condition your body so that your legs feel as fresh in the seventh inning as they did in the first inning. Include cardiovascular workouts at least four days a week in your training regimen.

WEIGHT TRAINING

University of Arizona conditioning coach Marc Hill once said, "Strength conditioning is not just simply for the benefit of getting big and strong, but also for being able to play at the highest level possible with as few injuries as possible."

Hill makes two excellent points in his statement. By increasing your strength, you're making progressive steps toward playing up to your maximum potential. That is what each player should aspire to achieve. The other important point made is that to perform well, you've got to be on the field. Weight training helps prevent injury. It strengthens muscle tissue, which protects ligaments and tendons. Without your health, you will unable to contribute to your team on the field. Facing a tough pitcher can give you heartache, but an injury puts you on the sidelines and takes you completely out of competition.

> **CONSULT WITH AN EXPERT**
>
> Many young athletes have not been educated in weight training exercises. If you're an athlete who has never been given strength training instruction, seek out a certified trainer or speak to your coach. As beneficial as weight lifting can be, it can cause injury if the proper safety measures are not taken. In addition, improper technique can bring about muscular strains and lead to chronic injury. Consult a professional to insure safety and reap the maximum benefits from your hard work.

Strengthening the body means the entire body. Isolating a few areas of the body and building muscle in those regions is short-sighted. The legs, torso, abdominals, lower and upper back, shoulders, chest, arms, and wrists all need to be built up. Because you're a softball player, give more attention to the legs, torso, abdominals, and forearms. Those regions are extremely important to this particular sport. That doesn't mean the other muscle groups should be ignored, but the exercises for those mentioned areas should be intensified.

Below are some basic weightlifting exercises. They are designed to strengthen and tone muscles, but not to build bulk. Building bulk can restrict your flexibility, which must be maintained for acts like swinging and throwing. Depending on what you may or may not have access to, Nautilus and Universal weight machines can work as substitutes for free weights. Seek the advice of a coach or expert before initiating your weightlifting program.

Recommending a specific weight-training program is a delicate topic when dealing with young athletes. Every girl has a distinct body type, physically develops and matures at different stages of life, and maintains a particular muscular structure due to her individual genetic make-up. We're unable give you an exact amount of weight for these exercises because too many factors like your age, strength, size, and weight are unknown. You are responsible for determining the proper and safe amount of weight for your workouts. As you'll notice in the exercises that are recommended below, it's suggested that you complete 10 to 15 repetitions for each set. Following this guideline, you should avoid using a weight that is too heavy. Beginners should increase strength through high repetitions rather than lifting heavy weights. As you mature physically and gain more strength, you can then increase the amount of weight and lower the number of repetitions. However, consult a certified trainer or coach before doing so.

Note: There are many types of strengthening exercises, far too many to list in this book. If you discover a program that includes exercises you don't recognize (or are not listed below), consult a certified trainer and request that they show you the proper technique.

Leg Extensions—Quadricep Muscles

Seated on a leg-extension machine, hook the tops of your feet under the pads. Lock your ankles, but don't point your toes. Extend your legs up so your thighs are flexed and your toes point to the ceiling. Slowly lower the weight back down until it's just short of the starting position. This keeps pressure on your legs throughout the exercise. Continue for 10 to 15 repetitions.

Leg Curls—Hamstring Muscles

Lying face down on your stomach, lock your heels under the pads of the machine. Point your toes to the ground. Contract your glutes and curl your legs up as far as you can. Isolate the hamstrings by keeping your hips and chest down on the bench. Lower the weight slowly just short of the starting position. Continue for 10 to 15 repetitions.

Lunges—Gluteus Maximus Muscles

Holding dumbbells (approximately 15–20 lbs.) in each hand down by your side, stand erect with your feet shoulder-width apart. Take a forward stride approximately three feet in distance. As your stride lands, bend your knee and lower your rear knee almost to the floor. Push yourself back up to the starting position and repeat with the right leg. Continue for eight to 10 repetitions.

Leg Press—Quadriceps, Hip Flexor, and Buttocks

Sit on a leg press machine with the soles of your feet flat against the foot plate. Slowly lower the weight down until the top of your calves touch the bottom of your hamstrings. Slowly push back up and stop just before your knees lock. Continue for 10 to 15 repetitions.

Bent-Leg Sit-Ups—Abdominal Muscles

Lying on your back, bend your knees in and place the soles of your feet on the ground. Place your hands behind your head and curl up, bringing your chest up to your knees. Continue for 20 to 25 repetitions.

Bent-Leg Sit-Up Twists—Abdominal Muscles

Lie flat in the bent-leg sit-up position. As you curl up, twist so your left elbow touches your right knee. Lower yourself back down and alternate

Sit-ups are excellent for developing strong abdominal muscles. Ask a teammate to hold your feet as you perform your sets.

by touching your right elbow to your left knee. Continue for 15 to 20 repetitions.

Leg Lifts

Lying flat on your back, lift your legs up off the ground (or bench) keeping both legs extended. Raise your legs until your buttocks lift off of the ground. Lower your legs very slowly until they are about four inches from the ground. Continue for 15 to 20 repetitions.

Medicine Ball Hand-Offs—Torso and Abdominal Muscles

You'll need a partner for this exercise. Holding a medicine ball, stand back to back with your partner. Twist to your right as she twists to her left and hand her the ball. Immediately twist to the left and receive a pass back from your partner. After approximately 15 exchanges, switch directions and pass the ball off to your left.

V-Seat Pull-Ins—Lower Back Muscles

Seated on the floor, extend your legs out in front of you and place the soles of your feet up against the foot plates. Lean forward with your upper body to grab the handle grips with both hands. Return to the seated position and allow you knees to flex slightly. Pull the grips into your midsection and stick your chest out as your arms touch your midsection. Slowly allow the weight to return to the starting position.

Pull-Downs—Upper Back Muscles

Seated on the pull-down machine, grab the ends of the bar with both hands, palms facing forward. Tilt your head slightly forward and pull the bar down behind your head until it touches your neck. Let the bar slowly raise back up and then pull back down. Continue for 10 to 15 repetitions. To alter the exercise and isolate the upper-back muscle region, flip your hands so that your palms face you. Pull the bar down in to the top of your chest and slowly return it to the starting position. Continue for 10 to 15 repetitions.

Bench Press—Pectoral Muscles

Lie flat on a weight bench with your feet flat on the ground. Grip the bar so your middle knuckles are pointed up to the ceiling. Each hand should be approximately three to four inches outside your shoulder. Lift the bar off of the rack and hold it over your chest. Slowly lower the bar until it touches the upper region of your chest. Keep your elbows under the bar. Push the bar back up until near extension. Continue for 10 to 15 repetitions.

Push-ups build upper body strength. A great thing about push-ups is that you can do them anywhere.

Bicep Curls—Bicep Muscles

Seated on the edge of a bench, hold a dumbbell in each hand. Rotate your wrists outward so your palms face forward. While maintaining an erect posture, slowly curl the dumbbell up near your collarbone. Lower the dumbbell back down and repeat the movement with your opposite arm. Repeat this 10 to 15 times with each arm.

Tricep Pull-Downs—Tricep Muscles

Standing at a pull-down machine, grasp the bar with both hands spread slightly narrower than shoulder-width apart. Use a forward grip so your palms face the floor. Push straight down on the bar until your arms nearly lock. Slowly let the bar return to the starting position. Continue for 10 to 15 repetitions.

Side Shoulder Raise—Shoulder Muscles

Stand straight up with your arms hanging down by your sides. Holding a light dumbbell in each hand, raise your arm out and up until it's parallel with the ground. When the dumbbell is at shoulder height, your palms should face the ground. Allow the dumbbell to slowly return to the starting position and raise the opposite arm. Continue with each arm for 10 to 15 repetitions.

DON'T FORGET TO BREATHE

Breathing is very important when training with weights. The body needs oxygen to fuel working muscles. Proper breathing during an exercise is very simple. Inhale during the relaxed portion of the repetition and exhale during the strenuous segment. For example, when doing pull-downs for the upper-back muscles, inhale as your arms are moving upward and exhale as you pull the weight back down behind your head. Inhale when you're relaxing and allow the weight to return to the starting position and exhale when you're pulling it back down.

If you don't breath, you'll have less strength and energy to complete your sets. You may even become light-headed and out of breath at the end of a set. Breath throughout the entire exercise.

AGILITY TRAINING

Diving back to the base on a pick-off attempt, running back to make an over-the-shoulder catch, turning a double play at second base, and charging into to field and throwing on a bunt attempt are examples of common plays that require agility. Speed allows a player to cover large amounts of territory in a small amount of time, but enhancing agility augments quickness, explosiveness, and the ability to change direction.

The following agility exercises are designed to improve your balance and quickness. They can be practiced right on the softball field. Coaches are often heard applauding players with a great first step, their ability to make cuts and sharp turns, or how fast a runner is able to accelerate. These exercises will help you develop those skills.

Lateral Line Jumps

Using the right-field foul line, stand on the foul-territory side of the line facing home plate. Place both feet together and position them so you're standing right next to the line. (Your feet are now parallel to the foul line.) Keeping both feet together, jump up and over the foul line, landing in fair territory. Without hesitation, jump back over to the foul-territory side, and continue jumping back and forth for 30 seconds. Do your best to maintain balance. Count how many jumps you perform in 30 seconds and work to increase that number each time you train. This exercise improves leg strength, balance, and explosiveness.

Forward/Backward Line Jumps

Turn your feet so they are perpendicular to the foul line and you're facing the outfield. Keeping your feet together, leap forward over the foul line into fair territory. Upon landing, immediately jump backward over the line into foul territory. Continue jumping forward and backward for 30 seconds. Count how many jumps you perform in 30 seconds and work to increase that number each time you train. This exercise improves leg strength, balance, and explosiveness.

Four Corners

Use four cones to set an imaginary square so that each cone sits at a corner. Each side of the square should be approximately 20 yards in length. Starting at the bottom-right corner of the square, jog straight to top-right corner cone. Once you reach the cone, shuffle sideways to the left along the top of the square. After reaching the top-left corner cone, run backwards down the left side of the square until you arrive at the bottom-left corner cone. Finally, sprint along the baseline of the square to return to the starting position. Continue this pattern until you've run four full circuits, and then rest. This exercise builds endurance and improves overall agility and balance.

Pick-Ups

You'll need a partner and softball for this exercise. Face your partner and stand approximately 10 feet away from her. Your partner initiates the exercise by rolling the ball about six feet to your right. Shuffle-step to your right, field the ball with your hands in the fielder's position, and then underhand toss the ball back to your partner. Quickly shuffle back as the feeder rolls the ball six feet to the left of your starting point. Continue shuffling back and forth until you've completed 30 pick-ups. Pick-ups improve lateral movement and leg strength.

Following Orders

Stand in the outfield grass or anywhere that gives you plenty of space. Face a coach or teammate and respond by moving in the direction of their command. Their job is to call out and point up, back, right or left. If the caller yells "back," backpedal until you're given the next command. If they point to your left and yell "left," shuffle to the left until hearing the next command. Continue following orders for 45 seconds before resting. This exercise focuses on your ability to change direction and also builds endurance.

To increase speed and explosiveness, run sprints before and after practice. Organize sprints with teammates to add excitement and competitiveness.

Bleacher Steps

You'll need a set of bleachers for this exercise. Stand at the base of the bleachers, raise your right foot, and place it on the first row. Your left foot remains planted on the ground as the ball of your right foot rests on the corner edge of the bleacher. This is the starting position. At the sound of a whistle or coach's call, interchange your feet as quickly as possible. Repeatedly exchange your feet, touching the front row of the bleachers with the bottom of your feet, "Left, right, left, right, left, right," etc. Continue exchanging feet for 45 seconds, accumulating as many touches as possible. Keep track of your total number and attempt to beat that number each time out. This exercise works on improving foot speed and quickness.

CONDITIONING PROGRAMS

How you train your body depends on the time of year and your personal goals. The off-season is the optimum time to build strength and increase speed. The lion's share of your work is performed at the fitness center or track, not on the softball field. Your ultimate goal is to improve as a softball player, but during the off-season, concentrate on developing a better body to execute softball skills.

Once you move into the pre-season, reduce your time spent at the gym, and begin focusing on softball. Instead of four or five work-

Exercise	Weight	Sets	Reps
DAY ONE			
Shoulder press	XX	3	8
Dumbbell bench press	XX	3	12
V-Seat Pull-ins	XX	2	12
Side shoulder raises	XX	2	10
Forearm curls	XX	burn	burn
Wall squats	XX	2	6
Leg curls	XX	2	12
Leg extensions	XX	2	12
Calf raises	XX	2	25
Abs (sit-ups)	XX	burn	burn
DAY TWO			
Bench press	XX	3	12
Power shrugs	XX	3	5
Dumbbell incline press	XX	3	10
Pull-downs	XX	3	10
Tricep extension	XX	3	10
Bicep curls	XX	3	10
Forearms (wrist rolls)	XX	burn	burn
Abs (leg lifts)	XX	burn	burn
DAY THREE			
Leg press	XX	3	12
Squats	XX	3	12
Leg curls	XX	2	12
Lunges	XX	2	6
Calf raises	XX	2	25
Medicine ball passes	XX	3	15
Forearm curls	XX	burn	burn
Abs	XX	burn	burn

outs per week, limit yourself to three sessions per week. Maintain your weight-training program, but adjust it by increasing the number of repetitions and decreasing the amount of weight. Cardiovascular, flexibility, and agility training exercises should be incorporated into practices by your coach. If insufficient time is spent in any of these areas, stay after practice and get your work in. Don't make the mistake of ignoring any facet of your conditioning program once pre-season starts. Your hard work in the off-season will be fruitless.

During the season, do your best to maintain strength and fitness. Lift light weights two or three times per week for approximately 30 minutes. These are classified as maintenance workouts designed to keep your muscles strong despite the wear and tear of a busy game schedule. The grind of practicing and playing every day causes the body to lose strength and explosiveness. Filtering in brief workouts helps to stave off weight loss and diminished muscle mass. Strenuous workouts are not recommended. Conserve your energy for competition.

Every player has a different body type, individual strength and goals so there is not one universal workout that is best for everyone. On page 193 is a weight-training workout program. Use this program as a foundation or guideline and then modify it to your personal needs and time of year. Set the weights at a comfortable level. This program is based on strength training three days per week. Always consult a fitness expert before starting to insure that your program targets the goals you're striving to accomplish.

Note: When the number of sets and reps is listed as "burn," that means you should continue performing the exercise until you burn out.

NUTRITION

You could own the sweetest car in school, but unless there's gas in the tank, it's not going to be of much service to you. The same theory applies when it comes to athletics. Athletic ability becomes a non-factor if your body is devoid of nutrients. Proper nutrition enables you to train or compete at the highest level possible. Eating the right foods fuels the body to perform at its best.

Eating properly allows you to maintain a desirable body weight, stay physically fit, and establish the optimum nerve-muscle reflexes. So is there something that I should eat every day that will satisfy my needs? Yes and no. There is no one specific food that will give you everything you need. Your body needs a variety of nutrients —proteins, carbohydrates, fats, vitamins, minerals, and water— to join forces to energize your body. Receiving all of these nutrients is accomplished by maintaining a balanced diet. The nutrient deficiencies in some foods are then overcome by nutrient surpluses in others.

To maintain a balanced diet, use the four basic food groups as your guideline. A combination of foods from the dairy group, meat and poultry group, fruit and vegetable group, and bread and pasta group provides a basic structure from which to devise your dietary plan. On page 195 is a table that lists the food group, the major nutrients each supplies, and the recommended amount for teenage athletes.

Food Group	Major Nutrients	Daily Servings
Dairy	Calcium, protein, vitamin A, riboflavin	3 servings

One serving is 8 ounces of milk, 8 ounces of yogurt, 1 1/2 ounces of cheese

Meat/Poultry	Protein, thiamin, riboflavin, iron, niacin, zinc	2–3 servings

One serving is 3 ounces of lean meat (poultry, pork, fish, beef), 2 eggs, 1 cup of cooked beans or peas, 4 tablespoons of peanut butter

Fruit and Vegetable	Vitamin A, C, and many other vitamins and minerals	5 to 7 servings

One serving is 1/2 cup of cooked vegetables, 1/2 cup of chopped vegetables, 1 whole fruit (apple, orange, banana), 1/2 grapefruit, 6 ounces of juice, 1/2 cup of berries

Bread and Pasta	Complex carbohydrates, protein, B vitamins, iron	6 to 11 servings

One serving is 1 slice of bread, 1/2 English muffin, 1 small roll or biscuit, 1/2 cup of cooked rice or pasta, 1 ounce of breakfast cereal.

Cleaning Up Your Diet

Young athletes often have poor eating habits largely because they eat what tastes best. Teenagers don't regulate their food intake as closely as adults do because there are often no visible results from eating poorly. Heavy involvement in physical activities and high metabolism negates the possibility of significant weight gain, giving the impression that their bodies are healthy. However, a book cannot be truly judged by its cover. Although your body may appear physically fit, it doesn't mean it's receiving all of the nutrients it needs to perform at its maximum potential.

Good nutrition is not just about eating the right things. It also requires you to stop eating the wrong things. If you are an athlete in search of improving your diet, here are popular poor-eating decisions to eliminate from your diet.

Avoid junk food. Tempering temptation is often difficult, but you've got to exhibit willpower if you're seeking results. Avoid snacks like cookies, potato chips, and cheese fries. Instead, keep some pretzels, bagels, and fresh fruit available.

Decrease your dairy products. Dairy products are one of the major food groups and it is suggested to include a mild amount of dairy (3 servings) in your daily diet. Keep it at that. Do not feed your hunger with cheeses, ice cream or sour cream-filled baked potatoes. Skim milk, low-fat yogurt, and low-fat mozzarella cheese are adequate replacements.

Ease up on the soft drinks. Soda and imitation fruit drinks are full of calories and provide very little supplements. They fail to quench your thirst or replenish your body with the energy it needs. Stick with water and natural fruit juices.

Drive past the drive-thru. Fast-food restaurants offer foods loaded with fat. If you must stop at a fast-food restaurant, look for menu items that are grilled and request that they leave the mayonnaise and secret sauce for the next customer.

Eliminate heavy toppings. Popular toppings such as butter, cheese, mayonnaise, heavy dressing, sour cream, etc. may add flavor to your meal, but they add even more fat grams. Fat-free dressing, mustards, vinaigrette, or low-fat margarine provide options to retrain your taste buds.

Eating before Competition

Eating the right thing at the right time can greatly benefit your competitive prowess. Your goal is to supply your body with enough fluids and energy to enable you to battle as hard as you can for as long as you need. Complex carbohydrates such as pasta, baked potatoes, toast, and cereals are highly recommended. These should be consumed approximately three hours before competition. Keep the portions small so that your meal is easily digestible. Because your emotions are riding high entering a game, your digestive processes may be slowed. Do not eat foods that contain a lot of fat, and avoid sugary foods as well. Fats are digested at a much slower rate and can make you feel sluggish. Sweets such as candy bars, soda, or honey may raise your blood-sugar level and reduce your energy level.

All-day softball tournaments can put you in a precarious position. Drinking plenty of fluids before and throughout the day is the most important issue to carry out. Consume a cup of cool water every 20 minutes during competition and 2–3 cups each hour after competition. Eat a meal heavy in carbohydrates the evening before competition, and feed yourself with snacks that are high in starch throughout the day's events. A box of granola bars would be a smart item to pick up en route to the tournament.

DO I NEED TO TAKE VITAMIN OR
MINERAL SUPPLEMENTS?

Athletes and parents of athletes are increasingly confronted with the issue of dietary supplements. The questions often raised are, "Will my athletic talents benefit from taking supplements?" and secondly, "If I'm not taking supplements, am I at a disadvantage to those who are taking supplements?"

Provided you work hard at your game, conditioning your body and eating properly, there is no need for vitamin or mineral supplements. Increasing nutritious foods to meet increased energy expended will supply more than enough vitamins and minerals. Experts concur that the basis of good nutrition is a well-balanced diet and vitamin and mineral supplements are no substitute for it. Excessive amounts of supplements taken over a prolonged period of time can prove to be harmful.

ORGANIZATIONS

National Collegiate Athletic Association (NCAA)
P.O. Box 6222
Indianapolis, IN 46206-6222
Phone: (317) 917-6222
Web address: www.ncaa.org

Amateur Softball Association (ASA)
2801 N.E. 50th St.
Oklahoma City, OK 73111
Phone: (405) 424-5266
Web address: www.softball.org

National Federation of State High School Associations (NFHS)
P.O. Box 690
Indianapolis, IN 46206
Phone: (317) 972-6900
Web address: www.nhfs.org

BIBLIOGRAPHY

Diagram Group. *Rules of the Game*. New York: St. Martin's Press, 1990.

Editors of Sports Illustrated. *Sports Illustrated 2000 Almanac*. New York: Time Inc., 1999.

Gola, Mark, and John Monteleone. *The Louisville Slugger Complete Book of Hitting Faults and Fixes*. Chicago: NTC/Contemporary Publishing Group, 2000.

Kanaby, Robert F. *2002 NHFS Softball Rules Book*. Indiana: National Federation of State High School Associations, 2001.

Monteleone, John, and Deborah Crisfield. *The Louisville Slugger Complete Book of Women's Fast-Pitch Softball*. New York: Henry Holt and Company, Inc., 1997.

Wukovitz, John. *The Encyclopedia of World Sports*. New York: Franklin Watts, a division of Grolier Publishing, 2000.

INDEX

Boldface page numbers denote major treatment of a topic. Those in *italics* denote illustrations.

A

abdominals **187–188,** 193
accuracy, pitching 101, 108, **110,** 122–123, 124
Achilles tendon stretch **180–181**
aerobics 184
agility training 179, **190–192,** 193
Amateur Softball Association (ASA) 1–2
angles, minimizing **131–132**
ankle stretch **180**
arm circle and release **108–109**
Around the Horn drill **64**
athletic position 16, 17, 38, 89

B

back **182–183, 188**
backhand flip 64
backspin 52, 73
balance 16, **37–38,** 40

ball(s). *See also* throws, throwing; *specific kinds of balls*
  backhanding the 57
  blocking **71–72**
  dirt 80, 91, 94
  drop **113–115,** 124
  linear movement to 24
  passed 136
  rules **8**
  top-spin 40, 42
  wind and 90
baserunning **125–146**
base(s) **3**
  backing up **91–92, 120–121**
  hits 134, 137, 152
  stealing **73–75,** 92, **136–138,** 156, 157, 170–172
basketball 185
bat, batter, batting **8.** *See also* bunting, bunts; hitters, hitting
  cage net 40
  catcher and 75
  choosing 14
  control 162
  on curveballs 115–116
  grip of 13–15, 42
  in hi-low drill 45
  hip rotation of 42–43
  illegal 7

  in Indian Softball 49
  line-up 4
  outfielders and 89
  pitcher and 99
  position 17
  rules **6**
  swing of 28–31, 40–41
  weaknesses of 34, **119**
  wrapping the 23
batter's box 6, 17
batting tee 27, 38, 43–44, 47
Below the Knees drill **124**
bench press **189,** 193
bent-leg slide **139**
biceps **189,** 193
bicycling 184, 185
bleacher steps **192**
blow-out 127
breathing 40, **190**
bunt-and-run play **155–156**
bunting, bunts **147–158, 165–170**
  baserunning and 134
  defense on **72, 76, 82, 83–84,** 92
Bunt into the Bucket **161–162**
Bustos, Crystl 82
buttocks **187**